THE HERITAGE AND VALUES OF

INC.

THE HERITAGE AND VALUES OF

INC.

JEFFREY L. RODENGEN

Edited by Jon VanZile
Design and layout by Sandy Cruz

Write Stuff Enterprises, Inc.
1001 South Andrews Avenue
Second Floor
Fort Lauderdale, FL 33316
1-800-900-Book (1-800-900-2665)
(954) 462-6657
www.writestuffbooks.com

Publisher's Cataloging in Publication

Rodengen, Jeffrey L.
    The heritage and values of RPM, Inc./
Jeffrey L. Rodengen; edited by Jon VanZile;
design and layout by Sandy Cruz. — 1st ed.
    p. cm.
    Includes index.
    LCCN 2001131592
    ISBN 0-945903-73-1

    1. RPM, Inc. 2. Protective coatings industry
— United States — History. I. VanZile, Jon. II
Title.

HD9999.C6464R76 2002   338.7'6679
                            QBI02-200578

Library of Congress
Catalog Card Number 00131246

ISBN 0-945903-73-1

Completely produced in the
United States of America
10 9 8 7 6 5 4 3 2 1

Also by Jeffrey L. Rodengen

The Legend of Chris-Craft

*IRON FIST: The Lives
of Carl Kiekhaefer*

*Evinrude-Johnson and
The Legend of OMC*

*Serving the Silent Service:
The Legend of Electric Boat*

*The Legend of
Dr Pepper/Seven-Up*

The Legend of Honeywell

The Legend of Briggs & Stratton

The Legend of Ingersoll-Rand

*The Legend of Stanley:
150 Years of The Stanley Works*

The MicroAge Way

The Legend of Halliburton

*The Legend of
York International*

*The Legend of
Nucor Corporation*

*The Legend of Goodyear:
The First 100 Years*

The Legend of AMP

The Legend of Cessna

The Legend of VF Corporation

The Spirit of AMD

The Legend of Rowan

*New Horizons:
The Story of Ashland Inc.*

*The History of
American Standard*

The Legend of Mercury Marine

The Legend of Federal-Mogul

*Against the Odds:
Inter-Tel—The First 30 Years*

The Legend of Pfizer

*State of the Heart:
The Practical Guide to
Your Heart and Heart Surgery*
with Larry W. Stephenson, M.D.

*The Legend of
Worthington Industries*

*The Legend of
Trinity Industries, Inc.*

The Legend of IBP, Inc.

*The Legend of
Cornelius Vanderbilt Whitney*

The Legend of Amdahl

The Legend of Litton Industries

The Legend of Gulfstream

The Legend of Bertram
with David A. Patten

*The Legend of
Ritchie Bros. Auctioneers*

The Legend of ALLTEL
with David A. Patten

*The Yes, you can of
Invacare Corporation*
with Anthony L. Wall

*The Ship in the Balloon:
The Story of Boston Scientific
and the Development of
Less-Invasive Medicine*

*The Legend of
Day & Zimmermann*

The Legend of Noble Drilling

*50 Years of Innovation:
Kulicke & Soffa*

*Biomet—From Warsaw
to the World*
with Richard F. Hubbard

NRA: An American Legend

TABLE OF CONTENTS

Introduction vi

Acknowledgments viii

Chapter I   The Beginning 10

Chapter II   Formulation of an Acquisition Policy 28

Chapter III   RPM, Inc. (The Holding Company) 38

Chapter IV   The Planning Process 48

Chapter V   The Learning Process Does Not Stop 60

Chapter VI   The Transformation Begins 66

Chapter VII   The First Billion 78

Chapter VIII   The Right Markets 88

Chapter IX   RPM Rising 100

Notes to Sources 116

Index 135

INTRODUCTION

WHEN FRANK C. SULLIVAN founded Republic Powdered Metals, the forerunner to RPM, Inc., in 1947, he had a fairly simple business credo: Hire good people, create an atmosphere to keep them, and then let them do their jobs. More than half a centure later, with its successor, RPM, Inc., at $2 billion in sales and in the hands of his grandson, Frank C.'s maxim is still very much alive, still a deeply felt conviction.

At one time, Frank C. Sullivan was likely the best salesman in the entire paint industry. But like all entrepreneurs, he wasn't content working for someone else. Instead, he wanted his destiny, and that of his large family, in his own capable hands.

From its very earliest days, Republic Powdered Metals was a successful company. Besides his desire to let good people do their jobs, Frank Sullivan also believed in sales. He considered the sales force to be the core of the company, and he offered educational opportunities at every turn. Frank's focus on his people was so relentless that colleagues and employees would recall his generosity, drive, and spirit six decades later.

In 1971, however, Frank C. Sullivan died unexpectedly. He had served as Republic Powdered Metal's president for twenty-four years, and during his tenure the company had never experienced a loss. Frank C. Sullivan's untimely death was a crossroads for both his family and the company he had built.

At the time, Tom Sullivan, one of Frank's sons, was deeply involved in company operations. With his father's permission, he and a friend, Jim Karman, had orchestrated several acquisitions of smaller coatings companies in the late 1960s and early 1970s. In doing so, they had grown Republic Powdered Metals to more than $11 million in sales in 1971 and gained valuable insight into the art of the deal. Tom Sullivan's approach to buying companies was very much like his father's approach to people: Find good companies, give them a reason to sell, and then stand back and let them prosper.

Tom himself, however, had an additional vision. Shortly after his father's death, he pulled together the company staff and announced that Republic Powdered Metals would go on but as a wholly owned subsidiary of new company, RPM, Inc. At the same time, he got together with Jim Karman and had an impromptu "executive committee" meeting. On the porch of Karman's house, they hatched a plan:

RPM, Inc. would grow to $50 million in five years, or Tom Sullivan would sell the company. It was audacious, but as Tom Sullivan remarked, "We've got to grow rapidly because everybody is going to be watching us."

Watch they did, in astonishment. Although in 1976 RPM actually fell $3 million short of its goal, it was good enough to, as Karman said, "start on our next goal." Over the next thirty years, Sullivan and Karman grew RPM by leaps and bounds, first past the $100 million mark in 1979, then the $1 billion mark in 1995 and the $2 billion mark in 2001. Earnings kept pace with revenue growth, and throughout this time, RPM established one of the best records of increased earnings and sales anywhere in corporate America. When *Fortune* magazine went hunting for CEOs of the decade in the 1990s, Tom Sullivan's name was on the list.

Sullivan and Karman built RPM through shrewd acquisitions, purchasing niche coating and paint companies throughout the industry. By the millennium, RPM owned such stalwart brands as DAP, Rust-Oleum, Day-Glo, and many, many others. And these companies had not been acquired only to be gutted and repopulated with RPM executives. Instead, RPM itself remained surprisingly small; Tom Sullivan trusted his operating presidents, letting them establish their own sales goals and methods and run their own businesses. RPM companies weren't forced into buying groups, they didn't seek synergies unless it made sense, and they weren't grouped into divisions on some phantom organizational chart.

This pattern—full of exciting individual stories—is really the prelude to the modern RPM, Inc. The story ends with the development of a new management team, as well as a new beginning for RPM, with the founding philosophy intact.

ACKNOWLEDGMENTS

A GREAT NUMBER OF PEOple assisted in the research, preparation and publication of *The Heritage and Values of RPM, Inc.*.

The principal research and narrative time line were the work of Jay Miller and Chrissy Kadleck. Jay's dedicated effort was invaluable, and Chrissy tracked down and collected the hundreds of images in the book.

Special thanks are also due to Tom Sullivan, chairman of RPM, Inc. Without Tom's generous donation of his time, insight, and memories, this book would not have been possible. Similarly, Frank Sullivan, president and CEO of RPM, Inc., helped develop the RPM story. Jim Karman, RPM's longtime president, also contributed his memories and insights for the narrative. Also, special thanks to Tom's wife of forty-two years, Sandra, who added personal aspects of Tom and the family. Along with Sister Maureen Doyle, Sandra placed special emphasis on Tom's activities in the near West Side of Cleveland.

Tom Sullivan's siblings and other relatives also lent colorful and important details to the story. The author's gratitude is extended to Jack and Sue Jacobus; Jim and Joan Livingston; Dave and Kaki O'Neill; Father Sean Sullivan; and Charles Harty Sullivan, Tom's uncle and godfather. Jim Karman's wife, Carol Karman, also contributed her memories.

Many other people connected with RPM, including past and present employees, well-wishers, and customers, also gave their time during extensive personal interviews. Each of them deserves special recognition. They include Marilyn Brace, former assistant to Frank Sullivan Sr.; Joe Ciulla, a retired accountant; Mary Hall Crawford, Tom Sullivan's longtime secretary; Robert D. Deitz; Glenn Hasman, vice president, finance and communications; Ulf Eriksson, president, RPM Belgium; Ken Evans, retired president, Consumer Group; Robert Fleming, former sales manager, Republic Powdered Metals; Jeff Korach, president, Tremco Group; John Mars, Tom Sullivan's guidance counselor at Culver Military Academy; Jay Morris, retired executive vice president; Julius K. Nemeth, retired vice president; Bill Papenbrock, a longtime RPM board member and friend of the company; Chuck Pauli, president, RPM II Group; Mary Ann Peterman, assistant to Glenn Hasman and with more than three decades of service to RPM; Sheryl Redick, receptionist at RPM for more than fifteen years; Dave Reif, president, StonCor Group; Kathie Rogers, manager, investor relations, and Jim Karman's assistant; Bob Senior, president, Zinsser Group; Mike Tellor, president, RustOleum Group; and Noreen Wendt in human resources.

As always, special thanks are extended to the dedicated staff at Write Stuff Enterprises, Inc.: Richard F. Hubbard, executive author; Jon VanZile, executive editor; Melody Maysonet, senior editor; Heather Deeley, assistant editor; Bonnie Freeman, copyeditor; Mary Aaron, transcriptionist; Barbara Koch, indexer; Sandy Cruz, senior art director; Rachelle Donley, Wendy Iverson, and Dennis Shockley, art directors; Marianne Roberts, vice president of administration; Bruce Borich, production manager; Sherry Hasso, bookkeeper; Linda Edell, executive assistant to the author; Lars Jessen, director of worldwide marketing; Joel Colby, sales and promotions manager; Rory Schmer, distribution supervisor; and Jennifer Walter, administrative assistant.

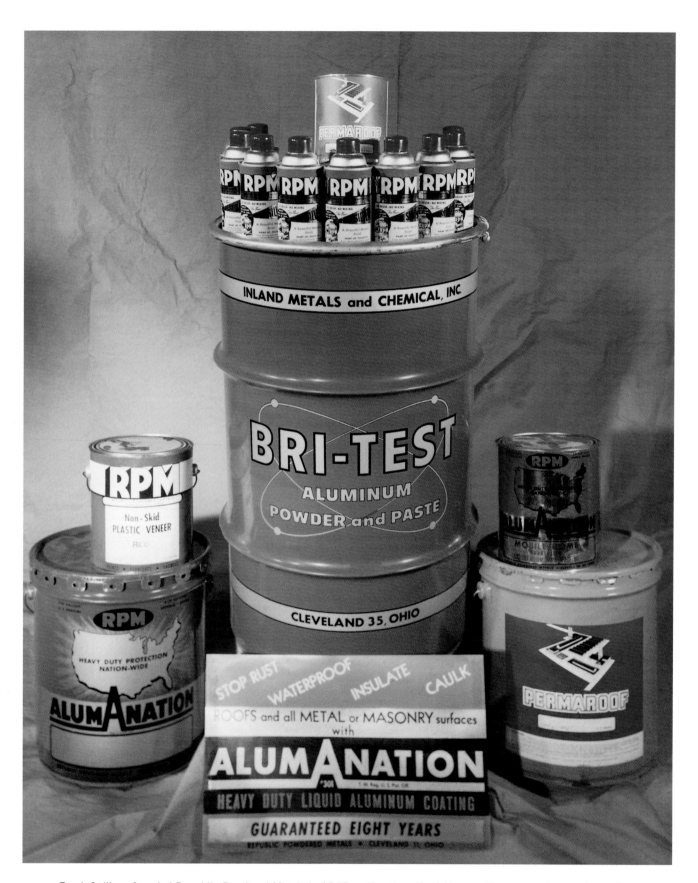

Frank Sullivan founded Republic Powdered Metals in 1947 on the strength of Alumanation, a premium roof covering.

CHAPTER ONE

THE BEGINNING

The spark that ignited the company to generate the longest-running streak of consecutive record years in sales and earnings of any publicly owned company. A history from the mailroom of a small Cleveland industrial paint company to the boardroom of one of the ten largest paint manufacturers in the world.

FRANK CHARLES SULLIVAN always wanted to be the best. As a mail boy for Cleveland's Arco Paint Company in the early 1900s, Frank C. would later boast to his family, he could run the few blocks between the Arco plant and the post office in six minutes—about half the time it took the other boys to cover the same distance.[1]

Young Frank landed the job at Arco through his father, Frank J. Sullivan, a first-generation Irish immigrant, who was described as a handsome version of the union leader, John L. Lewis. Unions, in fact, had figured prominently in Frank J.'s employment prior to Arco. Before entering the paint business, Frank J. had been an electric company lineman and a business agent for the International Brotherhood of Electrical Workers Local 39. In 1905, he was elected union treasurer and moved from Cleveland to union headquarters in Springfield, Illinois. He was new, however, to union politics and quickly became convinced that the union's leaders were mishandling the organization's business.

The Sullivan family was growing in these early years of the twentieth century. On January 21, 1906, Margaret Jamieson Sullivan, Frank J.'s wife, gave birth to Frank Charles. Before long, there were eight young Sullivans. Following Frank C. were Delphine, William, Edwin, Thomas L., Katherine, Charles, and John, who was called Jack.[2] All the

Sullivan boys except Charles would work in the paint business at some point in their careers.[3]

Frank J. was working in Illinois during the years most of his children were born, but by 1913 he wanted to return to Cleveland. "My father couldn't stand the crookedness of the unions," recalled Charles Sullivan. "I heard a story that at one point he had to carry a gun. The end came when he was away in St. Louis and my mother was home with little kids, and union officials approached her about asking her husband to do something they wanted him to do. That was the straw that broke the camel's back, to impose upon his wife. She was a young woman with babies."[4]

Frank J. put his wife and five children on a train for Cleveland and went to his final union meeting in Denver. In Cleveland, the large Sullivan family was met by a relative and given a place to stay until Frank J. could return. When he did, he landed a job at the Municipal Light Company and taught electrical theory at night at a technical school. But the family was struggling, leading

---

Frank C. Sullivan, pictured around the time he founded Republic Powdered Metals. At this time, he was already one of the best salesmen in the paint and coatings industry.

Frank J. to take a job at Arco, a paint company where his brother-in-law was divisional sales manager. A very young Frank C. began sorting Arco's mail part-time that same year.

The Nation's Coating Center

It was a good time to be in the paint business, especially in Cleveland. The midwestern city had established itself early on as the nation's leading center for paint production and development, and many of America's best-known paint brands had their roots in Cleveland. Some of this clustering had to do with luck, some to do with the emerging auto industry, and some with the oil industry.

In the early years of the Industrial Revolution, Cleveland merchant John D. Rockefeller was busy building his oil empire and its companion industry, the primary chemicals business. This offshoot of petroleum production supplied resources to the growing paint industry, and before long paint development was making headway. Paint historian George Heckel argued that paint and varnish research in the United States had its origin in "a group of bright young technical men, mostly graduates of the Case School [now Case Western Reserve University], at Cleveland, in the plant of the Atlantic Refining Co. . . . of that city."[5] Atlantic Refining, later called Arco, was founded in 1881 by Samuel Wise and became known for the development of synthetic paint resins.[6]

Around the same time the Arco labs were working on new paints, another powerful force began to emerge: the auto industry. Headquartered in Detroit and with factories spread throughout the Midwest, car manufacturers needed high-quality paints and pigments for their automobiles. In response, paint labs began to work on producing better-coating and faster-drying products.

By 1900, just before Frank J. Sullivan got into the industry, Cleveland was the undisputed national center of paint manufacturing, with twenty-three firms producing paints, varnish, and other coatings.[7] These firms, including Sherwin-Williams, Glidden, and Arco, acted as a fertile breeding ground for entrepreneurs, and soon many new, smaller paint manufacturers began to emerge. These included companies like Forbes Varnish (later purchased by PPG Industries), Gibson-Homans,

Master Mechanics, Tremco, Tropical Paint, and the Flood Company.[8]

Frank C. Sullivan Grows Up

In 1916, after three years working with his son at Arco, Frank J. quit for a job as eastern sales manager for Acorn Chemical Company, one of the smaller, entrepreneurial companies springing up throughout the city. Located on Cleveland's west side, Acorn Chemical (later Acorn Refining) was owned by Edward M. Katz and Samuel S. Sanders, former employees of Tropical Paint. The two had joined forces in 1906 to found Acorn, along with Issac Evans, who later left to form the Master Mechanics Company. (It is interesting to note that Tropical, Tremco, and Master Mechanics, renamed Mameco, would all become part of RPM).[9]

Frank C. stayed on with Arco for two years after his father left, then joined Acorn in 1918.[10] Still a boy, Frank C. spent most of his time in school and worked only part-time. He attended Saint Colmans, a Catholic elementary school, and then went on to Cleveland's West High School, graduating in 1924. Frank C.'s charismatic personality had already begun to be reflected in his achievements. In high school, he was president of his senior class, president of the honor society, and captain of the basketball team.[11]

A popular student, Frank C. formed friendships at West High that followed him throughout his life. George Karch, a high-school friend, later became president of Cleveland Trust Corporation and a director of RPM, Inc.[12] George Tinnerman, another high-school friend, became a leading Cleveland businessman.[13]

During his summers, Frank C. attended classes at the Culver Summer Naval School, an extension of the Culver Military Academy in Indiana. Besides setting in motion a lifelong association with the school, Frank C.'s time at Culver was important for another reason: during a graduation dance, he met Margaret (Peg) Wilhemy, the daughter of a local florist, and began courting her.

After high school graduation, Frank C. enrolled in Miami University in Oxford, Ohio. Yet he still didn't sever his ties with "the Acorn" (as the company was called by its employees). When he wasn't in class, he combed the towns and farms of southwestern Ohio selling Acorn products. During one memorable sales call, Frank C. tried convincing a dairy owner to buy Acorn's metallic coating because it was "just as good" as the brand the dairyman was currently using. After hearing Frank C.'s sales pitch, the farmer observed that the young man had a strange approach to sales, since the metallic coating he was currently using was "no damn good." The dairy farmer bought two drums of Acorn's Clevo Metallic Coating nevertheless, but recommended that Frank C. never again compare his product with his competitors'.[14] It was a piece of advice the young man heeded.

In 1927, after only three years at Miami University of Ohio, twenty-one-year-old Frank C. dropped out to take a full-time job with Acorn.

His reasons had less to do with the university than with his abilities. He was a natural salesman and realized early on that he had found his career. "He was probably the most dynamic salesman that I've ever known, and I have worked with many hundreds of salesmen over the years," observed Robert Deitz, an employee, competitor, and friend.[15] After Frank C. left college, he maintained a very close relationship with the institution and later served on its board of trustees.[16]

Frank Sullivan was captain of the Culver Summer Naval School championship basketball team. He is pictured holding the ball, wearing his letter sweater from West High School.

A 1923 picture of Frank C. Sullivan's class at Culver Military Academy. Sullivan is in the fourth row of the center section, fourth from the left. He became captain of his company, and his association with Culver would carry through the next two generations of Sullivans.

It was a busy time in his life. Less than a year after joining Acorn's sales staff full-time, Frank C. married Peg in a June wedding. They honeymooned in Canada, then moved into a house on Cleveland's West Side. Within a year, they were anticipating the birth of their first son, Frank C. Sullivan Jr., whom they nicknamed Sully. Five more children would follow: Margaret Patricia ("Pat"), Joan, Catherine ("Kaki"), Suzanne ("Sue"), and Tom.[17]

His Career Takes Off

As Frank C. established himself at Acorn during the late 1920s, powerful forces were brewing in the country. In late 1929, still settling into their new house, the family watched as the stock market jittered, swung wildly, and finally collapsed. The Great Depression had begun, and with it came shifting tides and uncertain times for many millions of Americans. The paint business, however, proved to be more resilient than some. Faced with expensive maintenance projects, many companies opted instead for a new coat of paint—at least until the Depression eased. Frank C. and the Sullivan family were fortunate and did relatively well in these years.

"We had a very happy upbringing," Sue (later Sue Jacobus) reminisced. "My parents were happy together. My dad traveled a fair amount, but when he was home, there was a lot of togetherness. Sunday afternoon was everybody lying on the floor reading the paper."[18]

There was also sadness in the home because Pat was ill much of the time. But the Sullivan family cherished mutual respect, a positive outlook, and a strong work ethic. Every morning, Frank C. got up and announced, "I wouldn't have missed this day for anything," Sue remembered. "That was his philosophy, and he meant it. He meant the weather. He meant getting up on your feet. He said that every day, and every morning in the shower he sang "You Must Have Been a Beautiful Baby." He was a very, very good father and a very good husband to our mother."[19]

In 1934, with the country still in the depths of the Depression, twenty-eight-year-old Frank C. was promoted to sales manager for Acorn's Midwest district. This promotion came with an unusual compensation: a contract in lieu of a salary entitling him to 30 percent of the company's profit.

Soon after, he became involved with the development and production of Uniflex, a heavy-duty, ready-mix aluminum roof coating. Uniflex was a novel product in many ways. At the time, most aluminum roofing paint was mixed at the work site. Uniflex, however, was an already-mixed product that could simply be applied as a waterproof, rust-proof, and heat-reflecting barrier.[20]

One of the first aluminum-fibered roof coatings, Uniflex was a popular product that Frank C. and his sales force pitched throughout the Midwest, actually driving up sales even during the Depression. Some of the sales managers Frank C. hired and trained in those years, like Louis Gillich, Bob Fleming, Julius Nemeth, and Ralph Tongue, would remain with him for many years to come.[21]

By the late 1930s and 1940, the Depression was easing somewhat, partially because of America's shift to defense production. In 1944, Frank C. Sullivan became Acorn's sales manager, with overall responsibility for the company's sales, third in authority after the company's owners. Recognizing that Acorn's strength lay in its heavy-duty protective coatings, like Uniflex, Cementseal, and Bardamp, Frank C. moved to slim down the extensive product line, which included forty different varieties of coatings.

World War II

Although age and family status exempted Frank C. from military service in World War II, the global conflict would ultimately have a profound effect on the Sullivan family and Frank C.'s career. Four of his brothers served in the armed forces, and Frank C. kept in close touch with them while they were overseas. "He was very interested in all of us,"

The Sullivan family, pictured in the 1950s. Standing, from left, are Sean (originally Frank C. Jr., called Sully), Tom, Frank, and Joan. Seated, from left, are Sue, Peg, Kaki, and Pat. The large family was extremely close, and all of the children worked in the family company at some point.

said Charles Sullivan. "He was the oldest. He was always sending nice things overseas."[22]

The war, in which the United States fought between 1941 and 1945, also represented a turning point for all of American industry, including the paint business. The military, operating in climates as extreme as the Sahara or the tropical Solomon Islands, had varied and extensive needs for protective coatings. Paints were needed to seal machinery from moisture and to help guide planes onto makeshift runways all over the world. Urged along by military spending that drove the paint industry to more than $1 billion in sales, manufacturers developed paints and coatings that were acid-proof, corrosion-proof, waterproof, fire-retardant, fungus-resistant, fluorescent, and phosphorescent.[23]

At the same time, scientists began to experiment with different pigment carriers. Until World War II, paint pigments were generally carried on an oil base. During the war, however, gasoline rationing and a petroleum shortage prompted scientists to look at alternatives. This effort was pushed along by military necessity. In North Africa, for example, where both oil and water were scarce, the Army needed a camouflage paint that could be diluted in any liquid.[24]

Naturally, though, the search for a new pigment carrier led quickly to water. It was readily available in most places, and if paints could be developed that were water-based, there would likely be considerable consumer demand after the war ended. Water-based paints cleaned up easily, and most homeowners could apply them easily. Before long, new water-based products were introduced, including Sherwin-Williams' Kem-Tone, which used synthetic chemicals to hasten application and drying, and The Glidden Company's Spred Satin, a latex paint that was washable and odor free. Sherwin-Williams even introduced the "Roller-Coater" applicator, which made it easy for novices to spread the new paints.[25]

When the war finally ended in Allied victory in 1945, the industry's investment paid off handsomely. Immediately after the war, with Europe and Asia in shambles, American industry was poised for a rapid and massive expansion around the globe. Domestically, after years of wartime deprivation, pent-up consumer demand was also poised to spark a business boom.

This was all good news for the paint industry. New production techniques and population patterns reshaped the domestic landscape as returning veterans and their families began moving in droves to a new creation: the suburb. Populated by single-family homes, suburbs were a paint-manufacturer's paradise. These new homes and the new kinds of paints lay the foundation for the do-it-yourself (DIY) paint industry. "The ranch-style home," noted *Modern Paint and Coatings*, "can be painted by the dweller with the help of a stepladder."[26] As new materials such as aluminum siding and stucco crowded into the exterior coating business, the DIY paint industry never slowed down.

Early Successes

Frank C. played a pivotal role in Acorn's success in these years of rapid growth. Between 1936 and 1946, Acorn's sales increased from $2 million to $8 million, doubling its size every five years—a pattern his son would follow years later. Uniflex was being used by the federal government to protect storage tanks.[27] Sullivan's formula for success was simple: Hire the best salesmen in the industry and

Above: Sullivan believed the success of a business depended on attracting and retaining good employees. Here, Sullivan, middle, is pictured with George Masterson, left, and a sales trainee.

Below: Acorn workers in Dayton applying Uniflex to the roof of the Biltmore Hotel in 1947. That year, Frank Sullivan founded Republic Powdered Metals.

let them do their jobs. He informed all of his managers that their job was to hire and motivate the salesmen and let them deal with customers. Frank C. was reportedly the highest-paid employee in the entire paint industry, and he exhorted his sales force through regular bulletins and meetings. One memorable memo to Acorn salespeople near the end of the war implored the sales staff to try new techniques when it came to selling.

> *We want to go into this post-war period with the best in the business and with a running start—this is why we want our men "blazing new trails" every day, because there is an old saying: "BEATEN PATHS ARE FOR BEATEN MEN."*[28]

But Frank C., who always wanted to be the best, wasn't truly satisfied with his success at Acorn. "I remember my dad talking about the fact that he and Frank would be chatting, and Frank would be dreaming of starting his own company," said Julius Nemeth, who went to work as an office boy for Frank Sullivan at age fourteen and whose father, Julius Sr., was factory manager at Acorn.[29]

Initially, Frank C. approached Katz and Sanders with an offer to buy Acorn, but they weren't interested. Although "they treated him like a son,"[30] the pair wasn't ready to sell Acorn to their star salesman. They had recently invited family members into the company and were preparing them to take over.

Undaunted, Frank C. decided to start his own sideline business. With Katz's and Sanders's blessings, forty-year-old Frank C. founded Basic Metals to sell aluminum pigment, not only to Acorn, but to all aluminum coatings companies interested in making a homogenized aluminum coating. Basic Metals would broker an exclusive agreement to market and distribute the aluminum pigment. Sales rose rapidly, and inside of a year, in 1947, Metals Disintegrating bought out Basic Metals for $43,000.

The Birth of Republic Powdered Metals

Flush with cash, Frank C. pooled his resources with his brothers', and, again with Katz's and Sanders's blessing, five or six former Acorn sales representatives formed Republic Powdered Metals.

Remarkably, Katz and Sanders paid Frank C. to remain as sales manager for Acorn despite the fact that Republic would be offering a competitive product line.

"They wanted the best of both worlds," Nemeth remembered. "They actually backed Frank for a short period of time. They were trying to keep him going at Acorn, where he was doing the best job of all the sales managers, and yet let him branch out on his own."[31]

In conjunction with the founding of Republic, the Sullivan family created Pliable Metals Corporation. Similar to Basic, Pliable would sell aluminum foil to Republic and other coatings makers. Frank's original plan was to have his oldest child, Sully, run Pliable as a complement to Republic, but Sully had other plans. A popular and handsome young man who was homecoming king at Miami of Ohio, Sully made a decision in his early twenties that shocked his family. While traveling overseas, he called home and announced that he was planning to enter the priesthood. Frank C. was disappointed that his eldest son wouldn't be going into the family business, but he and Peg gave positive support to their son's decision.

Sully changed his name to Sean, and his parents celebrated his ordination as a priest years later.

Republic Powdered Metals prospered, and Frank C.'s other children would work at the company at one time or another. "He thought it was important," Sue Sullivan Jacobus said. "At sixteen I worked as the receptionist, and I had to do the billing. The numbers had to balance, and that was scary because part of the time they didn't, and I was aware that others in the office had to help me. I was really placed down there to help my work ethic."[32]

Frank C. had large ambitions for his young company as well as for his children. At the time of its founding, he announced that he wanted to make his product, which he would call Alumanation, "the Coca-Cola of roof coatings"—"You can't win unless you think big," he would say.[33]

Republic Begins to Grow

Even after Republic had been founded and its main product began to compete directly with Uniflex, Frank C. stayed on at Acorn.[34] This left him with the monumental task of running both businesses simultaneously. He enlisted the help of his employees. Louis Gillich, who worked at both places alongside Frank C., later remarked that "he would run Acorn in the morning, then run Republic in the afternoon."[35]

Frank C.'s secretary, Marilyn Brace, made the move from Acorn to Republic in the company's very early days. "He was a great person to work for," Brace remembered. "He was a very kind, generous man, and he had a real drive about him for his work. He loved it, and he was a great salesman."[36]

Republic was destined to grow quickly. In 1947, its first full year of business, Republic registered sales of $88,000.[37] That year, Frank C. bought a piece of vacant land on the southwest fringe of Cleveland for $6,000, then

Republic's main products, circa 1960. The company relied on Alumanation as its mainstay for sales, although it also offered protective coatings for a variety of jobs.

The company's headquarters on West 150th Street in Cleveland. The building expanded rapidly as Republic grew. To keep his employees satisfied, Frank had the office buildings air-conditioned and offered a family-style cafeteria lunch.

Inset: Pat Sullivan, one of the six Sullivan children, greets employees at Republic Powdered Metals. All of the Sullivan children worked in their father's company.

paid another $4,000 to build a small manufacturing facility. Tom Sullivan, Frank's youngest son and the future leader of the company, would later describe the site, on West 150th Street, as "a dirt, country road."[38]

Marketing at Republic was directed primarily at the maintenance industry. Recognizing the intense competition brewing among paint giants in the DIY market for common house paints, Frank C. steered his company toward a market niche: roofing and maintenance products. The company's force of commissioned salespeople and manufacturers' representatives sold directly to property owners, roofing contractors, and industrial maintenance companies. Less than 10 percent of its business came from the new construction market.

Besides Alumanation, Republic also produced and sold a small line of maintenance coatings for customers in government, industry, and even racetracks—whoever needed a durable coating for roofs or metal or masonry surfaces. Finally, Republic's product line included Permaroof, a waterproofing coating, and Nu-Sensation, a masonry and concrete waterproofer that came in several colors.[39]

A People Person

Part of Frank C.'s success hinged on his recognition of a basic fact about his industry at the time: Companies like Republic Powdered Metals would never really be technological innovators. Most of the innovation in the paint and coatings industry took place in labs at petrochemical companies, or at least in much larger paint companies. Instead, Republic Powdered Metals would prosper by relying on its sales and marketing. "We were always told that the salesmen were the most important people in the company," remembered Bob Fleming, who joined Republic full-time in February 1958 as a division sales manager. Frank taught his managers to be totally "people focused."

In this respect, Republic already had an advantage. It had, after all, been founded by one of the best salesmen in the paint industry. Frank C. was directly responsible for creating the sales and marketing culture that fed Republic's rapid growth, through a philosophy that simply stated, "Go out and get the best people you can find, create the atmosphere to keep them and let them do their jobs." Employees and friends alike remember Frank C. as a charming, affable guy who was well-liked by everybody.

"He was a very, very personable, people-oriented person," remembered Nemeth, who joined Republic in 1952 as an assistant sales manager. "Frank was a master at talking to people. He really enjoyed people and worked well with them and as a result was able to get maximum results because people genuinely enjoyed working with him. He was not lofty in any way, and he was open to ideas and suggestions and encouraged them."[40]

But he was also known as a man who made his opinions clear. "The beauty of the man was if you did something wrong, you knew it right away and you knew it strong," remembered Tom. "The next day it was forgotten. Just don't repeat it. That was the rule."[41]

"He could make an example of someone," Fleming agreed. "But it was forgotten after that. He said that everyone is going to make mistakes, and just don't make too many. Very seldom in those days did anyone leave the company. Frank might decide to let someone go, which he very rarely did, but very seldom did anyone leave the company on his own."[42]

Sullivan tended not to view Republic's product as paint so much as people. He focused his efforts on training the best sales staff he could put together and keeping them happy and securely employed.[43]

By 1953, Republic had grown to a point that it demanded more and more of Frank Sullivan's time. Finally, at age forty-seven, he left Acorn for good to run his own company. As he left, he took some of the salesmen with him—again with Katz's and Sanders's consent—in exchange for his agreement not to raid the Acorn staff for five years.[44]

By this time, much had already been accomplished. The small facility at West 150th Street was expanded in 1949, ballooning from a twenty-five-hundred-square-foot plant into twenty thousand square feet of plant and office space. In keeping with Frank's attitude toward his employees, he had the entire office suite air-conditioned—an uncommon luxury at the time. He was so pleased by the results that the workweek was trimmed to thirty-five hours. "Our air conditioning has paid for itself many times over by increasing work

output and has certainly influenced our decision to shorten the work day to seven hours—in spite of the fact that our busy season is just ahead," Sullivan told an electricity industry publication in the spring of 1955. Sales by that time had climbed to more than $1 million.[45]

The same article also noted that Republic offered its employees amenities including music, a cafeteria that served a fifty-cent, family-style lunch to the company's fifty employees, free soft drinks, and transportation to bus lines. "Turnover is no problem with us," Sullivan said. "We believe that anyone who works happily can do a better job. Employee benefits tailored to that end go a long way to making an operation efficient, keeping it productive."[46]

Beyond the amenities, Frank C. also believed in personally vesting key employees in the company's success. He invited his best sales managers to buy stock in Republic Powdered Metals even while the company was still private. Nemeth was one of those invited into the company and remembered Frank C.'s generosity.

"I told him there's absolutely no way I can afford to buy stock because I had a baby on the way and a house mortgage," Nemeth said. "And he said, 'Well, I'll arrange a loan for you,' which he did with a local bank. But about every ninety days, the bank kept raising my rate. One day, Frank said, 'How is it going?' and I said, 'Well, it's fine, but those guys keep raising my interest rates.' He promised to fix that, so the company loaned me the money to buy stock in itself, which was a wonderful approach for me, as a young man, to be able to get an interest in a company."[47]

Selling Alumanation

Frank C. and his staff used a variety of techniques to promote Republic's products. He urged his staff to oversee their use because improper application created problems that reflected, unfairly, on his products. Frank C. often recommended that his salespeople keep copies of everything they'd ever written for reference, and he also saved memos and letters from customers. One of the earliest was a memo from Frank Cartille, a Republic salesman in New Orleans who received a letter from a grateful customer.

Dear Frank,

On April 23rd I completed a roof job on the House of Detention. That is, the work was done under my personal supervision. On April 24th, we had a 6 inch rainfall (a deluge accompanied by high winds) and not one drop came through.

This roof is a low-pitch, galvanized iron and has been leaking like a basket. I stripped all laps with Permaplastic and Alumafoil then coated the 40 squares with Alumanation #301. The city officials are very much pleased with the job, and I am very proud of it due to the fact that so-called roofing experts failed to stop the leaks. (It has a 4' x 48' parapet wall.)[48]

In 1955, Sullivan spoke to *Cleveland News* business columnist Jack Cleary about the company,

---

A 1960 sales meeting. Frank Sullivan, wearing the tan overcoat, standing second from left, believed that sales was the most important part of Republic.

marking perhaps the first time that Republic appeared in the mainstream media. Cleary quoted Sullivan's views on sales.

Many a company virtually drives itself out of business trying to cut corners in manufacturing processes in order to improve profit returns. My formula is to put greater effort and promotion into sales. The increased volume that results will more than compensate for the few pennies that may be saved through picayune economies in production techniques.[49]

Sullivan's practice of spreading "the gospel of the qualities of his company's product throughout the country" had, said Cleary, led Republic to outdo other coating companies in aluminum pigment use.[50]

In 1957, Republic Powdered Metals celebrated an interesting milestone when, in the words of Frank C., "The sales and profits of Acorn and Republic Powdered Metals crossed—Acorn on the way down and Republic Powdered Metals on the way up."

Before long, Acorn would be posting regular losses and would be sold to an investment group in New York. "The decline that took place at Acorn is something I really felt bad about," Frank later wrote. "Actually, after I left we were never in direct competition on too much business and certainly no competition for salesmen. This business is like all other businesses, it is a case of good management—it requires an intensive selling program and you have got to live the business seven days a week and as many hours every day as possible—I continue to work it that way."[51]

In fact, Sullivan's favorite number was 168, which is the number of hours in a week—the forerunner of 24/7.

From West to South

"Spreading the gospel" of Republic's products throughout the country was part of Sullivan's plan. With transportation improving and the United States fusing into one cohesive market, Sullivan wanted Alumanation to be part of the emerging national roof-covering industry. In 1959, he traveled to Hawaii and signed up the company's first major distributor outside the forty-eight contiguous states.

Two years later, to serve the growing western market, Sullivan negotiated for the purchase of a new plant in Gilroy, California, about forty miles south of San Jose. It was Republic's first satellite operation, and it opened in a logical region.[52] Republic already had good sales reps active in the

Three of Frank Sullivan's daughters pose during a 1958 trip to Havana, Cuba. Republic's products were used in the restoration of Morro Castle, an ancient Spanish castle and tourist attraction on Cuba's coast. From left to right are Pat, Sue, and Joan.

In 1964 Republic earned the President's "E" Award in recognition of its ambitious exporting program. President Lyndon Johnson, right, presented Frank with the award at a White House ceremony.

Before long, Sullivan himself was ready to visit this growing market. Cuban President Fulgencio Batista had begun the restoration of Morro Castle, an imposing and ancient Spanish fortress that was being converted into a training center. During the Morro Castle application, Sullivan took his wife and three of his daughters to Havana.[56]

Republic also established international distributorships. The company was among the first to use the St. Lawrence Seaway, a joint project of the United States and Canada that opened a waterway from Lake Superior to the Atlantic Ocean. From Cleveland, Alumanation traveled across the Atlantic to Belgium, where Sullivan had established an outlet. From there, Republic's products were sold to the Trans-Arabian Pipe Line Company in Beirut, the French auto company Renault, and the Ministry of Public Works in Hong Kong.[57] By 1962, Republic had registered sales in twenty countries.[58]

This ambitious overseas expansion earned the President's "E" Award in 1964, presented to Frank Sullivan by President Lyndon B. Johnson personally at the White House.

Sullivan and the IRS

In 1962, Sullivan gambled on the company's growing profile and took out an expensive advertisement in *Life* magazine seeking national sales agents. *Life* was then one of the biggest consumer publications in the country.

As it turned out, this ad generated a minor uproar when Frank reported it to the IRS as a business expense. At the time, Frank Sullivan was earning about $150,000 a year as a paint salesman and was a target of IRS audits claiming "unreasonable compensation." He withstood these audits because his accountant, Joe Ciulla, was able to prove that Frank Sullivan actually made less as an equity owner of Republic Powdered Metals than he had as a sales manager for Acorn. When it came to the ad, however, the IRS charged it "was not business related, that it was personally related."[59]

This charge was also easily trounced, or as Ciulla commented, "They didn't have any ground to stand on."[60] Within a year after running the ad, Republic had increased its sales force by 20 percent and added a substantial number of new clients.[61]

area, and there were good sources for both asphalt and solvents. Pigment paste, on the other hand, was shipped from Ohio.[53]

Sullivan was also pushing the company's products south toward warmer weather. As a reflective, waterproof roof coating, Alumanation was perfect for hot weather and tropical climates that had a long rainy season. In 1952, the head of the U.S. Naval Mission to Cuba, Commander R. C. Benitez, purchased some Alumanation and Permaroof for American installations in Cuba.[54] Six years later, Republic received a bid proposal from a Cuban architectural firm that was putting together a bid for a job at the U.S. Naval Base at Guantanamo Bay.[55]

Alumanation Farms

Indeed, Republic's revenue was rising quickly as its profile increased throughout its industry. In 1959, net income was $104,000 on sales of $2.1 million. By 1963, these numbers had risen to income of $109,000 and revenue of $2.9 million, respectively. All of this expansion resulted in Republic's first manufacturing facility outside of Ohio, with a new plant in Gilroy, California.

In 1962, Frank Sullivan began to hunt for land to accommodate his growing hobby of horse racing. He found what he was looking for while driving through rural Medina County, where he spotted a homemade "For Sale" sign that advertised "Land for Sale, Approximately 100 Acres—by Owner Only."

Sullivan had no intention of stopping immediately and introducing himself to the prospective seller while wearing a business suit and tie. Instead, he returned the next day, unshaven and dressed in old clothes. The property was owned by a gentleman named Clyde Buttoff, and he and Frank Sullivan signed an agreement to purchase the property on a kitchen napkin that Buttoff found in a kitchen drawer.[62] Like most agreements Sullivan made with individuals, a handshake was all that was needed. Later that afternoon, Sullivan received a phone call from Paul Jones, president of the Old Phoenix Bank, who said he hadn't seen anything like it since the 1930s. The transaction was completed in four days.

By the mid-1960s, with the West 150th Street plant growing cramped, Frank Sullivan began the task of relocating Republic to Alumanation Farms. This setting was both a factory and Frank Sullivan's racehorse-breeding operation.

In addition to developing a horse farm, Sullivan built a new $250,000 research and development plant called Inland Aluminum, which produced aluminum pigment.[63]

To accommodate a large breeding operation, Frank Sullivan founded another subsidiary called Alumanation Farms, which initially was owned by Republic Powdered Metals. Sullivan was a man of few hobbies who spent most of his time working. He once remarked that he wouldn't have anyone working for him who had a low golf handicap. But Sullivan loved horse racing and had been a regular attendee at the Kentucky Derby for years. By 1958, he had already begun investing in and breeding racehorses.[64]

Although Alumanation Farms, later called Brunswick Farms, would be peeled away from the corporation in 1968, horse racing and breeding would remain a lifelong passion. Mary Ann Peterman began working in Sullivan's stables during her sophomore year in high school and remained with RPM for the next thirty years. "I actually lived at the farm for a while," she said. "And Frank had the bunkhouse all fixed up for me with a refrigerator and everything. I never had to pay any rent, no phone bill, nothing. He'd ask me from time to time, 'Is there anything else you'd like down here?' And there wasn't. They were wonderful, wonderful people to me."[65]

Alumanation Farms was once described as "an immaculate thoroughbred showplace."[66] Speaking to a reporter, Frank C. remarked that, "I'd like to pattern it after Calumet Farms," a leading horse-breeding operation that produced many Kentucky Derby winners.[67] The best horse to live at Alumanation Farms was Te Vega, who won the 1968 Ohio Derby. Te Vega was called by longtime racing writer Isi Newborn "the most famous thoroughbred ever foaled in the Cleveland district."[68]

"I know that he enjoyed going out early in the morning to watch Te Vega work out at Thistledown [a racetrack in a Cleveland suburb]," Robert Fleming remembered. "I'd meet him out there now and then at six o'clock, and we'd watch the horse work out and maybe catch a quick breakfast and then be back in the office by eight."[69]

A New Sullivan Steps Up

Brunswick Farms, however, did not distract Frank C. from the job of running his company. He remained president and stayed intimately involved with the sales organization. But a new generation of leaders had already begun to rise.

Frank Sullivan with President Harry S. Truman. Sullivan was active in politics in addition to running Republic and managing a large racehorse-breeding operation.

Frank C.'s youngest, Tom Sullivan, became involved with Republic when just twelve, accompanying his father on a sales swing through Pittsburgh and New York. "He was a fun kid," Fleming remembered. "He did anything you asked him to do."[70] Tom officially joined Republic in 1961 as divisional sales manager.

In many ways, Tom Sullivan had traveled a path similar to his father's and had cultivated the same interpersonal skills that earned Frank C. such fierce loyalty. Tom even attended the same schools his father had gone to, including the Culver Military Academy.

"Tom entered Culver in 1951," remembered Col. John Mars, Tom's counselor there. "As a fourteen-year-old, Tom was already oriented toward self-discipline and doing what was necessary. He never had to be corrected, never had to be counseled. By his senior year, I used to turn things over to him, and he was my personnel officer. He dealt with kids who were in trouble. He would work with them as if he were twenty-four or thirty-four years old. He was only, at that stage, seventeen or eighteen."[71]

After Culver, Tom went on to Miami University of Ohio, where he was elected president of the freshman class and served on the University Senate during his four years. He graduated with a bachelor's degree in business and made the professional contacts that would serve him throughout his life. One of Tom's fraternity brothers, James Karman, would later become second-in-command at RPM.

After college, Tom Sullivan signed up with the navy and spent two years as a communications officer on a destroyer, USS *Braine* DD630, operating throughout the western Pacific. "That experience for us," said Tom's new wife, Sandy Sullivan, "living in San Diego and he being a twenty-two-year-old officer and having sixty people under him, was really a wonderful tool for learning to deal with folks. He had early leadership at an early age."[72]

Their first son was born during Tom's time in the Navy, and Sandy and Tom chose to name him Frank in honor of his grandfather. The couple, who met when they were teenagers, would ultimately have six children within an eight-year period. Like their grandfather and father before them, all of Tom Sullivan's children attended Culver Military Academy or Culver Summer Schools, and most began working for Republic at a very young age. The newest Frank Sullivan started in the family company when he was thirteen years old, working on the order desk over summer break.

"My dad worked really hard, and we had a really good childhood," Tom Sullivan Jr. remembered. "We were raised Catholic, and there's a strong sense of family values, sticking together as a team. I could trust my brothers and sisters or my parents with anything. Instead of flying off the handle, they'd think long and hard about it and then fly off the handle."[73]

In 1963, two years after Tom Sullivan joined the company, he recruited his college friend James Karman as chief financial officer. A native of Grand Rapids, Michigan, Karman had met Sullivan during the first week of their freshman year. They soon became pledge brothers at the Sigma Alpha Epsilon fraternity and were good friends throughout college; Tom Sullivan even introduced Karman to Karman's future wife, Carol. After graduation, while Tom was in the Navy, Karman attended the University of Wisconsin and earned his M.B.A. Tom approached him to ask if he would consider coming back to Cleveland and working for Republic Powdered Metals.

"He said, 'We're good at selling products, but we don't have a big strength in finance. I think we need somebody to help us with this side of the business,'" Karman remembered. "I knew it was a great company, and I knew his family."[74] Karman joined Republic Powdered Metals on January 2, 1963, setting the stage for what would become a strong partnership with Tom Sullivan over the next forty years.

REPUBLIC POWDERED METALS, INC.

Shining Example of one of the finest protective coatings in America. **ALUMANATION** is a product well known to maintenance men throughout America for its heat reflection and rugged durability.

$800,000 5½% SUBORDINATED CONVERTIBLE DEBENTURES

COMMON STOCK—25,000 SHARES
$8.00 per SHARE

ALUMANATION is a product of RPM Development and Imagination. It is one of the outstanding protective coatings in the RPM line.

The Republic Powdered Metals prospectus from the November 16, 1963, stock offering.

CHAPTER TWO

FORMULATION OF AN ACQUISITION POLICY

1963–1971

The early acquisitions were the most important in giving us the much-needed confidence to move forward on later acquisitions at Republic Powdered Metals.

—Tom Sullivan

TOM SULLIVAN AND JIM KARMAN shared a distinctive approach to Republic's business. Whereas Frank Sullivan had been the consummate salesman, training and motivating some of the most effective sales forces in his industry, his son and the new CFO believed that acquisition was the most effective way to grow rapidly in a consolidating industry, and they were eager to begin looking for good companies to buy.

Frank, of course, approved of acquisition as a business tool but was leery of siphoning energy from Republic. "His whole philosophy was, 'OK, if we're going to do acquisitions, I'm going to stay and make sure that Republic Powdered Metals was intact,'" remembered Tom.[1]

Nevertheless, industry-wide consolidation was unavoidable, and Frank put aside his early reservations. "I remember a conversation with Frank after the first acquisition closed," said Julius Nemeth, who had been promoted to executive vice president. "He had been getting some feedback with people saying, 'Gee, why are you doing this?' Everything was going well and Republic was providing a good income and did he really need the aggravation? But he said, 'My nature is I have to grow. I can't just sit here.'"[2]

Growth, of course, required cash. In 1963, Frank C. arranged a public offering of stock, but because of Republic's unconventional structure—the shares were to have no voting rights and the company owned a horse farm—underwriters wouldn't accept a national offering.

"I went to every stock broker in Cleveland trying to get them to take on the Republic Powdered Metals issue," Frank later said. "But it seems as though when one of them turns you down, the rest of them won't talk to you."[3]

Instead, several Republic employees, including Vice President of Sales Bob Fleming, Nemeth, Tom Sullivan, and Karman, were licensed to sell stock.

"We were having dinner on Sunday evening when the phone rang, and it was my father," Tom Sullivan remembered. "He said, 'Meet me in the office with your bags packed in an hour.' When I got there, Louis Gillich, Bob Fleming, and Julius Nemeth were there, plus Jim Karman, myself, and Dad. He said, 'We all have permission to go out and sell stock in the state of Ohio. Tom, I want you and Jim to go to Cincinnati and cover Cincinnati and Dayton.'

"Jim and I decided that we'd split up to cover as many brokers as we could," Tom said, "which

Tom Sullivan joined RPM's executive ranks with the idea of growing the company rapidly through acquisition. With his father's support, he began hunting immediately for good targets.

I always thought was a little unfair because he had a master's of finance degree and I had a master's of nothing. But I was smart enough to know that Merrill Lynch would not touch Republic's stock, so I figured, 'Well, I can go there because when I get rejected, I won't feel bad.'"[4]

Instead of getting thrown out of the office, however, Tom Sullivan ended up sitting down with the managing partner. Sensing his nervousness, the partner showed Sullivan how to read and promote a balance sheet and then recommended several local companies for him to visit. The first on the list was George Eustis and Company, billed as the "oldest bond house west of the Alleghenies." After one hour of talking with one of the firm's salesmen, Jim Martin, Sullivan closed an order for ten thousand shares with the firm (an $80,000 purchase, which ten years later would be valued at more than $1 million).

The office staff of RPM poses for a photo in the 1960s. Tom Sullivan's longtime secretary, Mary Hall Crawford, is standing fifth from left.

Republic's other impromptu brokers were having similar success, and before long the full allotment of twenty-five thousand shares of Republic Powdered Metals stock had been sold at $8 each. "We got (people) to commit to the purchase of shares," Fleming said in 2000. "A goodly number of shares were purchased by in-town people that Frank and I and Tommy were associated with at the Cleveland Athletic Club. A lot of them are still there."[5]

Moving to Medina

Some of this money was put to use immediately to expand operations. A proposed bridge on Cleveland's west side threatened to consume the West 150th Street location, leading Frank C. to the conclusion that operations needed to be consolidated and expanded at Alumanation Farms. In 1964, manufacturing operations were moved, doubling the company's thirty thousand square feet of production space.[6] Eventually, a fifty-thousand-square-foot can plant was added, and an A-frame sales and training complex called Beaver Lodge was built. Beaver Lodge offered sleeping, dining, and recreation facilities.[7]

Beaver Lodge, above, Republic's sales and training facility, was built on the grounds of Alumanation Farms. A group of salesmen, right, attend one of the training seminars at Beaver Lodge, which had all the amenities of home, including places to eat and sleep. Jim Karman is standing first from left, and Tom Sullivan is third from left, front row.

"It was a big move," said Marilyn Brace, Frank C.'s secretary, of the consolidation at Alumanation Farms. "But it was fantastic. You'd sit there at your desk looking out over the beautiful trees and fields. And the salesmen would come up to the lodge for meetings, and there were rooms where they could stay. Everything was right there, sales meetings, seminars, whatever Frank wanted."[8]

The Mode to Acquire

The physical expansion was necessary, but the infusion of cash was more important for another reason. Throughout the 1950s and 1960s, the paint industry was swept by successive waves of consolidation.

Because the growth of paint sales continued to lag growth in the gross national product, the best way for ambitious paint companies to grow was through acquisition.[9] The United States Census of Manufacturing tracked this trend through the 1960s. In 1963, the year that Republic went public, 1,579 paint companies were operating 1,788 plants. Less than ten years later, there were almost 400 fewer manufacturers and 200 fewer plants. Equally significant, eight paint companies, including notably Sherwin-Williams, Glidden, and PPG Industries, accounted for 35 percent of industry sales.[10]

Republic's corner of the industry, specialty and maintenance coatings, tended to be at the trailing end of the consolidation trend. While Sherwin-Williams and Glidden had begun consolidating the consumer paint industry in the 1950s, specialty and maintenance coatings remained largely outside the giants' notice. To the Sullivans, this translated into opportunity.

Using the money generated from the private sale of stock, Republic launched an acquisition program in 1966 that would push sales to $11.4 million within five years. These acquisitions helped shape the future of Republic Powdered Metals in very fundamental ways. Not only did the acquisitions expand the product line, but their success helped convince Republic's leaders that growth through intelligent acquisition was the way to build an industry leader.

Finally, the acquisitions foreshadowed the company's operating structure and its next generation of leadership. While Frank C. remained in the sales position he loved so much, the acquisitions were handled by Tom Sullivan and James Karman. Together, they perfected an approach that would form the backbone of a decades-long partnership.[11] Tom Sullivan, who had grown up in the paint industry, was "Mr. Outside," negotiating the deals and working with government and industry. Jim Karman, meanwhile, was "Mr. Inside," the finance and operations expert who made sure financing was in place and handled the day-to-day operational issues that arose. This partnership wasn't far removed from their relationship during college, when Tom Sullivan was elected to the Student Senate while Jim Karman remained active in dorm politics where he was president of Collins Hall. The partnership provided each man an arena in which he was comfortable.

"The learning experience surrounding the early acquisitions is perhaps one of the most important reasons for RPM's success in acquisitions today," Tom Sullivan later remarked.[12]

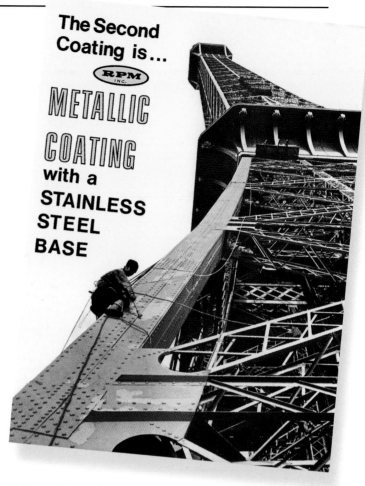

RPM metallic coating was used to protect the famous Eiffel Tower in Paris during its restoration.

The Reardon Acquisition

The first acquisition was the fortunate result of keen networking. Tom Sullivan and Karman began scouting around with investment bankers, looking for a company to acquire. Before long, they learned about the Reardon Company, a seventy-nine-year-old St. Louis corporation that specialized in the manufacture of Bondex, a waterproofing paint sold in liquid and powder forms.[13] It was owned by a loose consortium of business professionals, doctors, and accountants who would likely be receptive to selling.

The Sullivans, however, had no intention of calling Reardon because any show of interest would likely raise the cost of the company immediately. Instead, in 1966 they took out a targeted ad announcing their willingness to buy coatings companies. It didn't take long for representatives of the Reardon Company to come calling.

Reardon, best known for Bondex, had originally been a glue company but changed direction when it created a patented waterproofing paint for cement and concrete. The company also sold interior latex paint, basement paint, and a line of repair compounds.[14] Reardon had a Canadian manufacturing subsidiary in Montreal and an export arm, Bondex International Corporation. In addition to plants in St. Louis and Montreal, the company had shops in Los Angeles and Toms River, New Jersey.[15] It employed eighty-five people. In 1965, Reardon earned $179,000 on sales of about $4 million.[16]

Approximately the same size as Republic Powdered Metals, Reardon would almost double the size of their company if Tom Sullivan and Karman were successful.

It was a significant move, both for Republic Powdered Metals and for Tom Sullivan's and Karman's friendship, and the two young men were keenly aware of its gravity. They were following Frank Sullivan's philosophy of "thinking big." The night before the December 1966 Republic board meeting at which the acquisition would be presented, Tom Sullivan and Karman sat up on the roof of the old Kenilworth Hotel on Miami Beach until four in the morning, drinking two six-packs of beer and going over the deal.

Exhausted the next morning, they overslept and arrived late to the most important breakfast meeting of their youthful careers. Frank Sullivan shook his head furiously and shot the pair a piercing glare, then motioned them to two empty places at the table, where covered breakfast platters awaited them. Lifting the lid from his plate, Karman asked his friend, "What the hell is it?"

It was eggs and the most pungent and grisly looking Irish smoked haddock called finnan haddie. "I don't know," Sullivan replied, "but you better eat it."

After breakfast, the two received the go-ahead from the board to buy Reardon.

Reardon President Herman L. Brocksmith told the *St. Louis Post-Dispatch* that Republic paid $10 a share, or $2.3 million.[17] Much of the sale money was borrowed from insurance companies and the National City Bank of Cleveland.[18]

After the deal closed, Karman and Tom Sullivan moved ahead with their plan to overhaul Reardon and began visiting the company's various facilities. Sullivan later told a group at Case Western Reserve University what happened next.

In less than a year we closed their West Coast plant and stopped bidding on all government orders. The combination of this caused a loss of approximately $1 million in sales during the first full year. We also changed the compensation of the sales force from salary and expense to a straight commission and immediately lost a little better than one third of this group. I should say in our defense that the top third of that particular sales group doubled their earnings overnight.[19]

More ambitious than experienced, Tom Sullivan and Karman also addressed the company's man-

agement. About a month after they closed the deal, Sullivan and Karman traveled to Reardon's St. Louis headquarters. They figured the easiest and most equitable way to make any management change was to fire everybody at once, which they did in a single day.

After the job was over, Sullivan returned to Republic Powdered Metals, where he related the story to his father. "Dad came into my office, and I said, 'That was a nasty job.' He said, 'What do you mean? What's a nasty job?' I told him we just got back from St. Louis and we fired everybody. I'll never forget the look on his face. He said, 'Everybody? You fired the biller?' Now I knew I was in trouble, and I weakly answered, 'Yes, sir, everybody.' He said, 'Who's going to bill the orders to take them to the plant so that we can ship the orders, get paid for the orders, and pay for this acquisition?' Then he called me every name he could think of that wouldn't directly reflect on my mother or himself. Jim Karman came into my office, and he had that whole set of names he could use on Karman, and he did."[20]

After the tongue-lashing, Tom Sullivan stormed out of the office and went home.[21] That evening, Jim and Carol Karman dropped in on Tom and Sandy Sullivan only to discover there was a surprise party going on and a couple of neighbors were scattered throughout the house. A little while after that, Joan Sullivan Livingston and her husband Jim also showed up unexpectedly.

Shortly after the Karmans arrived, Frank C. knocked on the door, an unusual occurrence since Frank C. didn't often drop in on his children unannounced. When he got there, he saw what was going on and sat quietly in his chair rather than interrupt his son's social gathering. But he was seething and finally boiled over when Jim Livingston clapped Tom on the shoulder and asked, "So how's that new acquisition going?"

"My father sprang up out of his chair," Tom remembered, "and he called us everything he had called us earlier that afternoon."[22] Sandy Sullivan also remembered what happened: "He said, 'I don't care what it takes! Go back and rehire that person because you don't even know what the invoices are! Nothing! You don't know anything!'"[23]

Tom went into the office the next day, a Saturday, and met Frank C., who handed him a legal pad and told him to list every key position

Seated on the couch with Frank Sullivan, second from right, are three of his favorite salesmen from left to right, Bob Seidler of North Dakota, Bill Matthews of California, and Elmer Dunn of Louisiana. On the floor are Tom Sullivan, left, and C. Robert Wilhelmy, right.

in Reardon and who had held it. Then he told Tom to call them all back and offer them their old jobs.

"For the next three days we were running around trying to rehire the biller and a few other people essential in getting orders to the plant so we could ship to our customers," Sullivan said. "We were successful in rehiring some of these people at twice the salary they had earned previously and approximately one-half the productivity."[24]

Within eighteen months, however, the business was moved to Cleveland and placed under the supervision of Nemeth. Once again, Republic Powdered Metals was to learn a lesson about how to pull off a successful acquisition. Reardon, it turned out, operated very differently from Republic

Powdered Metals. Instead of making products to fill confirmed sales orders, as Republic had done, Reardon had to keep a full inventory of finished products on hand. "That was a complete departure for us—to have dollars wrapped up in finished goods inventory," Nemeth remembered. "But it was a good learning experience."[25]

But Republic Powdered Metals had already misstepped once with Reardon and was determined to stick with the company's successful strategy. In the future, this hands-off approach would become a trademark of Republic Powdered Metals' acquisitions. Whenever possible, existing management of a successful business was kept in place, and Republic Powdered Metals would only rarely try to change the company's operating philosophy.

The Briggs Bros. Paint Company Acquisition

In the 1968 annual report, Frank Sullivan remarked on the company's consecutive years of record earnings, saying, "Competition is very keen in the coating industry but with aggressive selling, quality products, and well-planned distribution, we have been able to maintain an after-tax profit that is much higher than the industry in general and among the highest of individual companies in the industry. We are continually looking for well-suited acquisitions."[26]

It wouldn't be long before the company found one. In 1969, Tom Sullivan and Karman found a regional paint company, figuring that such companies were ripe for acquisition as bigger companies like Sherwin-Williams and Glidden squeezed into their territories. The company was called Briggs Bros. Paint Company, a fifty-two-year-old Nashville, Tennessee, manufacturer that sold paints and coating throughout the mid-South. In 1969, Briggs Bros. registered sales of $835,000 and earnings of $85,000.

For this deal, Karman traveled to Nashville and dealt with a local realtor who was empowered to make the deal. The pair soon arrived at a price, one which Karman and Sullivan believed was favorable to Republic, and Karman headed to the closing meeting with his down-payment check in hand. There was an unpleasant surprise waiting for him. The realtor had apparently thought the deal looked so good that he matched Republic's offer and bought Briggs himself before Karman had the opportunity. Six months later, he turned around and sold the company to Republic at 50 percent above the original asking price.

It was a hard lesson on the importance of a standstill agreement giving Republic exclusive negotiating rights for a reasonable period of time, but it was also one well heeded. In the future, Sullivan and Karman would try whenever possible to offer preemptive bids on companies, hoping to lock in a sale price before the company went up for auction on the open market.

For his part, the owner of Briggs remained president of the company for several years despite his about-face on the sale.[27]

Mac-O-Lac Paints

The same year, Tom Sullivan and Jim Karman negotiated the acquisition of Mac-O-Lac Paints of Detroit. Another regional paint company, Mac-O-Lac sold a complete line of paints throughout Michigan and the Midwest. Founded in 1930, the company had annual sales of about $3 million and boasted earnings of $225,000 in 1969.

The Mac-O-Lac deal was a legally complicated one that took more than a year to finally close. "That was one that Frank C. dropped out of right away," Karman remembered. "We kept up the negotiations, and they kept quitting in the middle. Then they'd come back and say we haven't done it yet. It went on and on."[28]

Finally, however, the deal was closed, and Tom Sullivan and Karman departed for the closing meeting. Karman was carrying a $3 million cashier's check in his briefcase to complete the transaction. When they arrived at Mac-O-Lac's offices, however, Karman realized he had left his briefcase on the airport bus. They hurried back to the terminal and fortunately found the briefcase with the check intact.

Walter L. Field, president of Mac-O-Lac, retained his position after the deal closed.[29]

Three in a Year

By 1971, young Sullivan and Karman were becoming more confident with acquisitions, and Republic Powdered Metals' defining characteristics were becoming more and more sharply drawn. The company was known for performing rapid due diligence with a team of accountants ready on short notice to begin their work. Joe Ciulla, Frank C. Sullivan's long-time accountant, became Republic's outside auditor in 1964, and continues in that position today.

"We were able to do a very fast job as far as reviewing and coming to a conclusion for a complete due diligence," Ciulla said. "My job was first to review the financial statements to find out if they were accurate; second and most important, to determine what adjustments would happen once they were part of Republic Powdered Metals; and third, to project the cash flow and earnings. Every projection that we made and report that we submitted was pretty much the way we said it would be."[30]

In 1971, Republic Powdered Metals continued its streak by successfully negotiating for three companies. One deal actually closed the next year.

The first was F. O. Pierce, a Long Island company with about $3 million in sales.[31] F. O. Pierce

RPM representatives inspect aluminum that will eventually be used in the company's flagship Alumanation. Jim Karman is second from left, and Tom Sullivan is fourth from left, with RPM plant manager Sam Gerace at the far right.

sold mostly architectural paints along the East Coast. In what was becoming a familiar pattern, Pierce's management, led by Herbert E. Hillman, continued to run the new subsidiary after the company joined Republic.[32]

A Philosophical Framework: The Birth of RPM, Inc.

Besides dramatically increasing Republic's size, this first group of acquisitions helped Tom Sullivan and Karman form the approach to acquisitions that would guide them and Republic Powdered Metals, Inc., for the next three decades. Besides a hands-off operational approach, preemptive bidding, and speedy due diligence, Tom Sullivan and Karman had put together a series of five financial guidelines for any acquisition:

1. The target should be in a related industry;
2. The company should have a strong balance sheet;
3. The company should have pretax earnings of 15 percent or more;
4. The company should have good prospects for future growth; and

5. The company should have sound managers who would remain with Republic Powdered Metals and embrace Republic Powdered Metals' philosophy and enthusiasm for future growth.[33]

In addition to the financial guidelines, a Republic Powdered Metals philosophy toward acquisitions was being formed and would play the most important role in the company's acquisition program going forward. It followed very closely on Frank Sullivan's people philosophy—go out and find the good companies, create the atmosphere to keep their management, and let them do their jobs. In addition, Sullivan found it was far easier and much more productive to start with a "fair price" and not a "negotiating price," which quickly became well known throughout the industry.

In 1968, anticipating a national public offering, Republic Powdered Metals sold Alumanation Farms to Frank Sullivan. At that time, it was renamed Brunswick Farms.

In 1969, to further solidify Republic Powdered Metals in the midst of the acquisitions, the company declared a 3.5-for-1 stock split, followed by a national stock underwriting that was completed in September and raised $1.6 million.[34]

During the offering, Tom Sullivan and Jim Karman were reintroduced to an old college friend named William A. Papenbrock. In the decade since they had known each other at school, Papenbrock had earned his law degree and was practicing law at the Cleveland firm of Calfee, Halter & Griswold.

"At the first business meeting, I walked into the room, and lo and behold, there were Tom and Jim," Papenbrock remembered. "It was a successful underwriting, but they still had some problems—the horse farm, the IRS, things like that. My partners solved most of these, and I think Sullivan and Karman weren't too happy with the lawyers they had hired to handle it. It wasn't working for them."[35]

Shortly after the offering, Tom Sullivan and Karman fired their lawyers and hired Papenbrock's firm to represent Republic Powdered Metals in future acquisitions, working closely with Joe Ciulla to determine the legal and financial viability of any acquisition.

"Joe and I worked as sort of a combat team," Papenbrock later said. "Tom would call up and say, 'Pack your bags.' A lot of times, we would try to complete the deals in thirty days from start to finish. If we were buying a company, whether it was dealing with a public company or a privately owned company, we always tried to give them an

Ulf Eriksson was hired by Frank Sullivan in 1964 to help RPM build its overseas presence. Before long, Eriksson had put together a large Scandinavian operation.

agreement that we felt was fair from the get-go as a starting basis for negotiations."[36]

The money from the public offering was also used to expand manufacturing in Medina; Toronto; Gilroy, California; St. Louis; New Jersey; and Montreal.[37]

By the mid-1960s to 1971, Republic Powdered Metals received special export honors from both President Kennedy and President Nixon for efforts in developing international markets, principally in Japan and Europe. The Japanese market was opened initially in 1960 through a distributor, Onoda Construction Materials, who for more than forty years would remain a major customer of RPM products. The European market was opened through the efforts of a young Swedish man, Ulf Eriksson, hired by Frank Sullivan in 1964. The Scandinavian market, through Ulf's efforts, grew rapidly to the point that by the mid-1970s, Republic Powdered Metals was the largest importer of roof coatings to those markets. Having sold his businesses to a major Swedish company in the late 1970s, Ulf finished his noncompete clause and rejoined RPM in 1980 to spend more than twenty-five years developing new markets for RPM's waterproofing and flooring products throughout Europe.

By 1971, with revenues of $11.25 million and record earnings of $617,000, Republic Powdered Metals, Inc. had changed a great deal. Tom Sullivan and James Karman had almost tripled the size of the company by acquiring new product lines and companies. The future appeared very bright for Republic Powdered Metals and architectural coatings. These initial acquisitions not only provided a wonderful learning experience and developed the criteria used for the first acquisitions, but most importantly, they gave the young management team the confidence to "think big" in an acquisition program—a strength that would be greatly needed in the immediate future.

The year, however, was to toll a solemn note when the company lost its founder and "strong coach."

Tom Sullivan's family in the 1970s. From left are Sean, Kathleen, Sandy, Frank, Julie, Tommy, Tom, Danny, and Dan the dog.

CHAPTER THREE

RPM, INC.
(THE HOLDING COMPANY)
1971–1976

The business success and activities of Frank Sullivan can best be summed up by the fact that since founding RPM in 1947, he never experienced a loss and also knew nothing but continued increases in sales and income in his 24 years as president of RPM.

—Tom Sullivan, 1971 annual report

FRANK C. SULLIVAN, FOUNDER OF Republic Powdered Metals and at one time probably the best paint salesman in the business, died in his sleep on August 18, 1971.

He died in his home on the shore of Lake Erie after spending his final years selling Republic products and visiting his beloved horses at Brunswick Farms. The night before he died, Charles Sullivan, his brother and the only Sullivan brother who never worked in the paint business, called Frank C. to see if he could drop by for a visit. "He said, 'I haven't been feeling good, and yeah, I'd like to see you,'" Charles Sullivan remembered. "I went down and he looked wonderful."

The next day, Charles got a call from his niece Kaki, who told him that Frank C. had been found dead in bed.[1]

Tom Sullivan Steps Up

Frank Sullivan's death stunned Republic. "It came so quickly," remembered Noreen Wendt, who started her thirty-year-plus career with the company in 1968.

"It was really a family-type thing with Frank around. At lunchtime we'd walk down to the barns and pet the horses. Frank loved being out in the country—he always wore his high boots— and he was very generous to everybody in the

office. [His death] was a real, real shock to everybody."[2]

In the opening pages of the 1971 annual report, Frank Sullivan was memorialized eloquently by his son, Tom Sullivan.

Frank Sullivan was not only a great man, but also a great teacher, and over the past several years developed the finest management team and sales organization in the protective coatings industry.... His memory and principles will serve as a great inspiration for our future growth and success.

Frank C.'s death left Republic Powdered Metals without a founder, but not without a leader. For the decade preceding Frank C.'s death, Tom Sullivan had assumed ever more responsibility at Republic Powdered Metals, and at the age of thirty-four, he was prepared to step into the leadership role. He possessed many of the same characteristics that had made his father so effective. Tom had grown up in the business, and he was an affable person who was known for being

A Dean & Barry truck. Purchased in 1978, Dean & Barry was a regional, retail paint company. It was part of a 1970s strategy to diversify RPM into the retail paint business.

down-to-earth and hardworking. Like his father, Tom Sullivan was family oriented, had a strict work ethic, and was a superb salesman.

"It was a crisis," remembered Tom's sister, Joan. "But he closed everything off as far as outsiders except for the really, really trusted people. He had wonderful advice, and he had a lot of good, loyal people that stuck with him."[3]

Also fortunately—especially for a family-run company—there was no internal squabbling among Frank C.'s children regarding who would run Republic Powdered Metals. Tom was the solid choice. Shortly after his father died, Tom called a staff meeting and announced that "We're going to go on." Wendt recalled him saying, "This is what my father would have wanted us to do, and we're going to move forward."[4]

Tom's announcement pulled the company together after a great loss, which was important to

everybody who attended that meeting, and the company's veterans remember feeling secure in Tom's leadership. Tom himself, however, had his own grieving process to go through. He had just lost his father, his boss, and his business mentor. Sue Jacobus recalled driving to the funeral with her younger brother. "Tom and I happened to be driving to the cemetery alone," Jacobus said. "He had to stop the car and put his head down. He was in his early thirties and had six little children. It must have been so overwhelming."[5]

Back at the company, Tom Sullivan articulated his plan for the future. He wanted to keep growing and remain viable in a rapidly consolidating and competitive industry. It was necessary to move quickly to earn the respect of other companies and an investment community that might assume that an RPM without Frank C. Sullivan wasn't Republic Powdered Metals at all.

"We had to grow more quickly or we would lose credibility, since we had just lost the individual most closely identified with the company, and we had to get more publicly known," Tom said. "The night my father was buried, I went to

---

Frank Sullivan in October 1970, displaying the license plate that illustrated his work ethic (24 x 7 = 168).

In 1970, Republic Powdered Metals earned the President's "E" Star Award, given by President Richard Nixon for superior performance in foreign marketing. From left are Bob Wilhelmy, Tom Sullivan, Louis Gillich, Jeri Bonk, Laureen Skortz, Ralph Tongue, Don Holter, and Jim Karman.

Karman's house to pick up my children. Jim said, 'I'll do anything you want me to do. If you want to stop acquisitions and circle the wagons, I'm behind you 100 percent.' I said, 'No, we've got to grow and grow rapidly because everybody is going to be watching us.'"[6]

That same night, the two began to lay out their plans. They got together at Karman's house for an impromptu "executive committee" meeting and, sitting on Karman's front porch, agreed on a goal of achieving $50 million in sales by 1976 or else selling the company.

It was a bold plan, but it was necessary. Immediately after Frank C.'s death, the company's stock "sunk like a rock because people didn't think

Tom would be able to do what my grandfather did," said the younger Frank C. Sullivan, Tom's eldest son. "My dad grinned and made it happen."[7]

To attain faster growth through acquisitions within the coatings industry, management decided to form a holding company called RPM, Inc.

"Making it happen" in 1971, however, was far easier said than done. At the time Tom Sullivan assumed control of RPM—with investors all over Ohio dumping the company's stock—the national economy was floundering amid high interest rates, skyrocketing oil prices, and runaway inflation. This unique set of business circumstances, dubbed "stagflation" by economists, was brought on by a threatened OPEC oil embargo and high unemployment. Once again, though, RPM actually benefited during the hard times because of the nature of its products. Similar to Acorn's experience during the Great Depression, RPM found a ready market of people who would rather touch up something with new paint than go through costly upgrades and replacements. The same was true for businesses.

"Most corporations are leaning toward preventive maintenance on their existing facilities," Tom Sullivan told the media. "And the high rate of unemployment means a lot of people are sitting around the house with nothing to do and many of them will end up working on their homes, again for preventive maintenance purposes."[8]

The State of the Business

By this time, RPM was also at least partially protected from domestic recessions by its overseas operation. In 1970, the company was awarded its second major presidential award, this time the President's "E" Star Award given by President Richard M. Nixon. The award, which RPM was one of the first dozen companies and the first paint company to receive, recognized American corporations for superior performance in foreign marketing.[9]

During the award luncheon, Tom Sullivan said, "RPM feels that this selection carries with it a responsibility and we are confident that we can carry out this responsibility by an even more vigorous pursuit of our own export programs."[10]

Toward this end, in 1971, the company augmented its Belgian operation with warehouses in England, Sweden, Norway, Germany, Australia, and Nigeria.[11] Products from these warehouses were sold throughout the world by manufacturers' representatives and sales agents.

Domestically, RPM continued to refine its manufacturing. The original Cleveland plant was closed, and manufacturing capacity at Gilroy was doubled. New capacity had also been added through the acquisition of Briggs Bros. and F. O. Pierce, which operated plants in Nashville and Long Island, New York, respectively.[12] A year later, a new plant was constructed for Briggs Bros. in Knoxville, Tennessee. The plant introduced a new brand name line of paints called "Big Orange," picking up on the colors of Knoxville's University of Tennessee.[13]

The acquisitions also changed the way RPM sales operated. The smaller, regional companies—Briggs, Mac-O-Lac, and Pierce—operated independent stores that catered to the DIY architectural business. While this wasn't a business that RPM had traditionally pursued, the recognized brands boasted established sales. Experimenting with the idea of retail sales, in 1971 Sullivan opened three branded stores in Nashville.[14] The stores' concept, however, was expanded beyond the architectural DIY business, and they were also stocked with maintenance products.[15] Alumanation, the company's original maintenance product, continued to be the most important revenue producer.

Shortly afterward, RPM closed another deal that had been years in the making. The Sullivans had been courting Frank D. Pabis, founder and president of Mohawk Finishing Products, for several years. Pabis had founded Mohawk in Amsterdam, New York, in 1947 as a furniture repair shop. After a couple years, however, Pabis developed a line of furniture repair finishes and varnishes that became established in their narrow field.[16]

The negotiations took so long because of a price difference. Pabis wanted about $3 million for his company, but Tom Sullivan and Jim Karman had a lower figure in mind. As Sullivan recalled:

As soon as you tried to talk him down to around $2 million, he'd change the subject. He'd never say no. He'd just look at you and say, "Let me show you what we're doing out on the West Coast now." It finally dawned on us that he wasn't going to change. Well, over that period of time, the earnings grew to a point that justified our formula, which generally was ten times after-tax earnings.[17]

In mid-1971, Pabis and Tom Sullivan tentatively agreed on a price of $3 million in cash. To close the deal, Karman and Sullivan arranged to meet the Pabises in New York City. As they were having cocktails in the bar at the Waldorf-Astoria Hotel, the bar manager told Tom Sullivan that he had an important phone call. His wife was on the phone, urging him to come home because his sister Pat was gravely ill and near death.

Tom's reaction was emotional. "I sat in the middle of the Waldorf lobby with Jim Karman—and Connie and Frank were sitting at the table looking at us—tears streaming down my face, saying I had to go home," he remembered. "My sister passed away about a week later, and I thought, 'Well, I just blew that acquisition because if they ever thought "Here's an unstable situation," that scene confirmed it.' And God love Connie Pabis, because she told Frank that he couldn't turn back."[18]

The deal was successfully closed. Within six months, Sullivan and Karman added to the line of furniture finishes with the $225,000 purchase of H. Behlen & Brothers, another New York company that produced furniture paints, stains, shellacs, and varnishes. In the interest of efficiency, the manufacture of Behlen's product line was moved to the Mohawk plant in Amsterdam, though Behlen maintained its separate sales force.

In the fall of 1971, for estate reasons and to help pay for the Mohawk acquisition, it was decided to move toward a secondary stock offering early in 1972. Tom Sullivan recalled the situation.

It was a beautiful day in October when we were walking down in the Wall Street section and past the Merrill Lynch office. I said to Jim, "Let's go in and see if we can talk to Don Regan," the then-chairman of Merrill Lynch. We were stopped by the receptionist, who asked if we had an appointment. We indicated that we did not, but were sure that Mr. Regan would be interested in a company that was growing from $11 million to $20 million and was looking to do a secondary underwriting of its stock. The confused receptionist left his desk and came back a few minutes later indicating that Mr. Regan was "behind closed doors" but their vice chairman, Mr. Winthrop Lenz, would be happy to see us. After telling the RPM story, Mr. Lenz got in touch with Felix Davis, who covered the

Above: Jim Karman and Tom Sullivan had worked out a partnership that played to each man's strength. Karman handled financial angles while Tom negotiated deals.

Below left: Lunchtime at RPM. Beginning with Frank Sullivan, RPM offered its employees a cafeteria lunch with high-quality food. This program is a fondly remembered morale booster.

Midwest and who would arrange for an underwriting if, in fact, RPM's sales were headed towards $20 million. [19]

After that call, they passed the Kidder Peabody office on Wall Street, walked in and received an unannounced appointment with Al Gordon Sr., who later became an RPM shareholder. It was Don Miller who later convinced Sullivan that, given the company's size, they would be better off working with G. H. Walker, where Don was then vice president of corporate finance.

The underwriting was successfully priced on March 16, 1972, Peg Sullivan's birthday, at $23.25 per share.

RPM Expands Its Board; OPEC Erupts

It was a busy first year for Tom Sullivan, who was still adjusting to his role and tending to daily business. That year, Sullivan and Karman found time to make only the Behlen acquisition.

A Dean & Barry outlet. By the late 1970s, because of a steep rise in the price of raw goods, Tom Sullivan recognized that RPM could not compete effectively in the retail business. Dean & Barry and the other regional paint companies were divested.

Most of their time was spent pulling together the existing operating companies and honing their growth plan. Sullivan and Karman, sticking with the holding company structure, wanted to create a corporation that specialized in paints and coatings, that grew through acquisition of strong and independent-minded companies directed from a central corporate office, and that was a lean, formidable competitor in many related markets. They needed to move quickly to boost confidence in RPM and show that they could indeed carry on what Frank C. had begun.

To help add credibility to their efforts, Sullivan and Karman, both still in their thirties, began in 1972 to assemble a board that could provide them with expert advice. At the annual meeting, Donald K. Miller was elected to the company's board of directors. The next year William A. Papenbrock was named a board member. Still practicing with Calfee, Halter & Griswold, Papenbrock also served as general counsel.

The duo also began to streamline the management function at RPM. Although the operating companies would operate with considerable autonomy, Sullivan and Karman organized RPM around several related industries and promoted internally. Herbert E. Hillman, president of F. O. Pierce, was named group vice president for consumer products. Frank Pabis was named group vice president for specialty products. Both were also named to the board of directors.

By early 1973, RPM was beginning to assume the shape and form that later observers would recognize. And it didn't happen a moment too soon. After two years of instability, the national economy deteriorated with sudden finality. For RPM, which had a history of performing well during downturns, the situation was especially difficult because, after threatening for two years, the oil-producing OPEC nations finally collaborated to raise the price of oil to absurd levels. The stock market swooned even further as gas lines formed around the country; RPM's share price dove to $8 from its $23.25 level at its secondary offering on March 16, 1972.

"Prices of some of our raw materials literally doubled in a month's time," Tom Sullivan said. Some prices shot up even more. "Asphalt went from 17 cents per gallon to 34 cents per gallon. Aluminum went from 30 cents a pound to more than a dollar a pound. I can remember finding out that we were selling some products below cost."[20]

Getting Out of Retail

The steep price hikes hurt most in RPM's fledgling architectural market. The regional companies, which were competing on a local basis with paint giants for consumer business, suddenly found their profit margins vanishing. Even if they were continuing to sell paint, they couldn't compete with the massive leveraged purchasing power of much larger companies.

By the mid-1970s, Tom Sullivan was arriving at the conclusion that RPM should phase out its architectural paint business. In 1978, RPM actually bought one more regional paint company, an Ohio firm called Dean & Barry, but only because Dean & Barry already owned its own retail stores. This venture was short-lived. By 1985, RPM would be out of the architectural paint business for good.

The decision wasn't an easy pill for Sullivan to swallow. The architectural paint business was by far the biggest and most recognizable aspect of his industry, and by phasing out that portion of the company, he was tacitly acknowledging that RPM couldn't compete with Sherwin-Williams and Glidden, both based in Cleveland. Nor did the giants offer any consolation. During a business luncheon in the mid-1970s in Cleveland, Tom Sullivan ended up sitting near the chairman and CEO of Sherwin-Williams.

"I was at a lunch with some of the captains of industry hosted by David Rockefeller, chairman of Chase Manhattan Bank," he recalled, "and Walter Spencer, then of Sherwin-Williams, was there, and somebody was kind enough to mention RPM's record year that we'd just completed, and Spencer looked at me, and he said, 'Oh, you make that asphalt crap, don't you?' I got two speeding tickets back from downtown Cleveland to Medina because I was so mad and frustrated."[21]

Reorganizing for a New Future

Despite the setback in the architectural market, Sullivan and Karman moved ahead with their plan to build up RPM's existing businesses. These included specialty coatings and the bread-and-butter maintenance products. As always, Sullivan figured that corporate growth would come as a result of acquisition and internal development. The company, through its operating units, would drill deep into specialty and maintenance markets.

RPM entered another niche market later that year through the acquisition of Floquil-Polly S Color Corporation of Cobleskill, New York. Truly a targeted company, Floquil specialized in coatings used by adult hobbyists who made recreations of military and historical scenes. Floquil products were solvent based and used to protect model railroads, airplanes, and ships. Polly S–brand products were water based and used for similar purposes. Floquil President William L. Solotar remained with RPM.[22]

With the growing line of specialty products and the corporate move away from architectural paints, RPM reorganized once again: Floquil joined Mohawk; Republic Powdered Metals and its international sales operation comprised the maintenance products business; and the regional paint companies made up the retail products portion of the business. The Maintenance Products Division, led by Alumanation #301, continued to be RPM's biggest revenue producer. In 1973, it introduced Nu-Tex #555, a heavy-duty textured maintenance coating that sealed and hid defects in masonry.[23]

That year, RPM also purchased Gates Engineering Company, which made elastic membrane coatings for roofs, and corrosion-resistant tank liners. Gates's Neoprene and Hypalon products, sold under the GACO brand, were used on the cables on the Chesapeake Bay Bridge, at Dulles International Airport, and at Madison Square Garden.[24]

In 1976, RPM purchased Richard E. Thibaut, Inc., for $1.25 million. Thibaut was a ninety-year-old wall covering firm headquartered in New York City. Herman G. Kugler, who spent his entire professional career at Thibaut, stayed on to run the company under RPM.[25] Tom Sullivan believed wall coverings would complement RPM's existing businesses and could be distributed through the same channels. Thibaut had annual sales of about $5 million.[26]

Toward $50 Million

By 1974—one of the rare years in which RPM didn't acquire any companies—the U.S. economy had begun to stir, and there was a sense that the country had recently turned a corner after difficult days. That summer, President Nixon resigned from office as the Watergate political burglary undermined his presidency. Gerald Ford became president and immediately pardoned Nixon. American troops had come home from Vietnam, and finally the threat of oil shortages receded and the economy began to recover.

Throughout this domestic turmoil, RPM had grown steadily. Between 1973 and 1974, sales rose 26 percent, from $25.42 million to $32.03 million. The next year, sales rose another 11 percent to $35.42 million, and in 1976, RPM posted a single-year rise of 33 percent in annual revenues, to $47.23 million.[27] These solid financial results extended RPM's record of consecutive increases in sales and earnings to twenty-nine years.

Perhaps more emotionally satisfying than even this impressive record, however, was the vindication of Tom Sullivan's leadership. His hard work, his long hours away from his young

The 1974 Christmas party at RPM headquarters. Tom Sullivan is sitting in front of the RPM and Republic Powdered Metals' staffs, which shared offices.

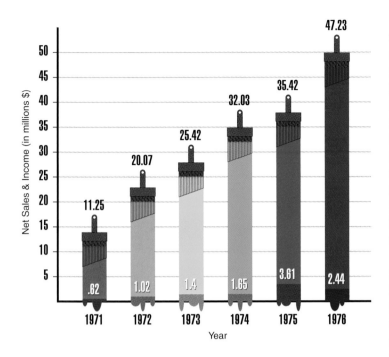

RPM's sales and income from 1971 to 1976. Earnings are represented by the darker area within the sales bar.

family, and his tireless efforts to attract the same caliber of people his father had recruited

were paying off. *Barron's*, a weekly Wall Street observer, declared in its July 28, 1975, issue that a "Broad Mix of Protective Coatings Adds Luster to Results of RPM." The magazine reported that the company ranked among the top fifteen of the fifteen hundred paint firms in the $15 billion paint industry. RPM ranked near the top of its industry when measured by revenue increases, earnings increases, profit margins, return on sales, and return on equity. "Bolstered by a more robust business climate, RPM should be able to extend its winning streak," noted the magazine.[28]

A year later, the *Cleveland Plain Dealer* reported that RPM was indeed heading for a record in its thirtieth year by sticking to its tightly focused expertise in maintenance markets and avoiding the architectural market, which "can be highly cyclical and price sensitive," Sullivan told the newspaper. RPM at this time had seven hundred workers in twenty plants and sold its products through a force of five hundred sales or manufacturers' reps worldwide.[29]

Ultimately, by 1976, RPM had fallen less than $3 million short of its ambitious $50 million goal. "We figured we were close enough," Sullivan said, "so we started on our next goal."[30]

Near the end of the 1970s, RPM's pace of acquisition slowed. Mameco International was one of its largest purchases.

CHAPTER FOUR

THE PLANNING PROCESS

1976–1979

If RPM was a person, it would be jolly, classy, honest, loyal, and people friendly. It would be a good citizen.

—Mary Hall Crawford, Tom Sullivan's long-time secretary

THE NEXT GOAL WAS NO LESS ambitious than the first. In 1976, Tom Sullivan and Jim Karman presented a new set of long-term target revenues to the board of directors and operating presidents. This time, they wanted the company to achieve $100 million in sales by 1981.[1]

The investment community, already pleased with RPM's performance through the recession, was thrilled with the new goals and happy to show it. Laury Jones, chairman of Van Dorn Industries, had a conversation with Jim Karman that would have long-lasting effects. "You really ought to go to the National Association of Investment Clubs," he told Karman. "Go to their national convention, and then be sure to go back every year."[2]

Karman did attend the National Association of Investment Clubs (NAIC) convention that year—and every year afterward as RPM forged a lasting relationship with the loosely affiliated group. Because of their fondness for stability and loyalty, values shared by RPM, the clubs became some of RPM's most stalwart supporters. In early 1976, the NAIC's local chapter heard a leading stockbroker, M. R. Covington of McDonald & Company, recommend RPM for his "millionaire's portfolio."[3]

Then in December 1976, *Better Investing*, the monthly magazine of the NAIC, put RPM and a handful of its products on the magazine's cover. In an article headlined "A Stock to Study," the maga-

zine declared, "RPM seems to be a case where the growth is produced by the drive and skill of management. The management team of Thomas C. Sullivan, president, and James A. Karman, executive vice president, is under forty and should have many vigorous years ahead of them to lead the corporation in continued growth."[4]

It also didn't hurt that Sullivan could tell the investment community that RPM demonstrated a sustained and dramatic increase in shareholder value.[5] RPM in 1975—and again in 1976, 1977, and 1978—declared a 50 percent stock dividend. In addition, the company continued to pay a five-cent-a-share quarterly dividend. An owner of 100 shares valued at $5,408 prior to the 1975 stock dividend would, by the end of 1977, own 338 shares valued at $18,252 and be receiving a 20 cent dividend per share annually.[6]

Setting RPM Apart

In late 1976, RPM announced plans to build a two-story, $250,000 headquarters building in Medina

By the 1978 annual meeting, Tom Sullivan was able to show steady, sustained growth under his leadership, and the company was reaching for $100 million in sales by 1979.

County. The plan called for a Georgian building set back a half mile on the Brunswick property. Corporate staff would be housed in a new building on the rolling green campus.[7]

Besides being logistically important because the corporate staff was running out of room, the new headquarters was psychologically important. "We found that we were really getting in the way of the operating companies," said Jim Karman. "We knew we were in the way because they were growing rapidly."[8]

By 1977, the move was complete.[9] When the new headquarters opened, officials described the building as a showcase for the company's products. While the building's exterior was largely brick, F. O. Pierce, Briggs Bros., and Mac-O-Lac all provided paints. Thibaut wall coverings sheathed some of the interior walls. Other company products were used less visibly: Bondex provided the spackling, and Gates and Republic Powdered Metals products protected the roof.[10] When some of the furniture for the new offices arrived with slight damage, workmen used Mohawk touch-up products.[11]

Over time, the new building would grow to be RPM's emotional headquarters, hosting employee picnics, traveling salesmen, and visitors. Its beautiful and serene setting was often remarked upon by visiting media and analysts, and the employees who worked there thought of themselves as a large extended family. Mary Hall Crawford, who joined RPM in 1962 and would be Tom Sullivan's secretary and office manager for more than

In 1976, RPM launched construction of this Georgian-style headquarters building in Medina, Ohio. Located among rolling fields and woods, the headquarters used many RPM products.

twenty-eight years, remembered how the small corporate staff enjoyed RPM's atmosphere and its seven-and-one-half-hour workday.

"We had a good atmosphere," she said. "We treat people nice, and we treat them with respect, and we in turn get the same thing back from them. If RPM was a person, it would be jolly, classy, honest, loyal, and people friendly. It would be a good citizen."[12]

By the time RPM had settled into its new quarters, Tom Sullivan believed that the worst of the recession was over and that RPM would maintain its high profit margins into the future. During the recession, RPM had benefited from its maintenance products; after the recession, Sullivan predicted that there would be a dramatic increase in consumer spending on home upgrades, furniture, and other products that used RPM's coatings and sealants.

Planning for the Future

Until this point, RPM had done little corporate planning because everything happened at the operating-company level. Very entrepreneurial executives, usually founders of the businesses, ran the operating companies, and they were comfortable—and successful—with Sullivan and Karman keeping their distance. In turn, Sullivan's friendly disposition and trust in his operating presidents inspired a fierce loyalty, and management turnover was very low.

But as RPM grew, it became apparent there needed to be some kind of official oversight. One day during the 1970s, for example, Karman was on the phone with Frank Pabis, the very independent president of Mohawk Finishing Products, when Karman heard a rumbling in the background that sounded familiar. It sounded like bulldozers, and Karman was curious to know what was going on. Pabis said he had decided to double production capacity and had committed $1.5 million to the construction of two new buildings. Karman was shocked and began to ask a few questions. Pabis cut him off by asking, "What do you want me to do? Tear them down?" The buildings stood.[13]

In 1977, RPM's board of directors began to lean on Karman and Sullivan to hire additional management. "We fought that forever," Karman remembered.[14] But as fortune would have it, just about that time John "Jay" Morris called Karman

looking for a new job. "He was with General Tire, and he wanted to get back to a good, small company," said Karman. "So I came back from a management meeting, and Tom said, 'Why don't you interview him?'"[15]

The interview went well; within a couple months, Sullivan and Karman had expanded their two-person executive committee by one, hiring Morris as director of marketing, then rapidly promoting him to vice president of corporate planning. Morris's charter was to create a planning strategy that fit into RPM's existing business model. He was qualified for the mission: in addition to a master's degree from Case Western, his background included stints as a planner at divisions of two rubber companies, first Armstrong and then General Tire & Rubber.

"I joined January 3, 1977," Morris said. "The corporate office was Tom, Jim, and the two secretaries. I can remember asking Tom where the economist was. Where's the guy that heads up advertising? Where's your market research director? He just kind of looked at me and said, 'I think that's going to be you.'"[16]

This was quite a challenge for Morris but signaled an even greater change for RPM. "Until then, planning was something that took place in the minds of Tom and the presidents of the operating companies," Morris told a reporter in 1992. "They usually managed to come pretty close to hitting their projections, but I felt we ought to try to formalize the process."[17]

Morris began slowly, first by developing a planning document. Designed to be filled out by each division president, the planning document was just a couple of pages that asked what their goals were for the coming year. "It was kind of, 'Who are you and how did you get where you are and what are you going to do for the next year,'" said Morris. "We wanted to institute a very gradual but very effective planning process."[18]

Starting slowly was imperative because Morris, then thirty-four years old, knew he had to tread carefully. "Had I gone in and said, 'You're going to be graded and your bonus is going to be based on this and your earnings and your gross profit margin, etc.,' I'd have ended up in the Delaware River," Morris later remarked.[19]

Most of the operating company presidents were older than he was and had owned their businesses and run them successfully before selling to RPM. Robert Wahlstrom, for example, was then in his seventies and had run Bondex International in Canada without any planning process for years. When he and Morris sat down to discuss the new process for the first time, Wahlstrom was courteous but clearly unhappy. "He looked at me after I did my presentation and said, 'Gee, I really question the relationship your parents had the day you were born,'" Morris said.[20]

Frank Pabis, president of Mohawk, was likewise skeptical initially. "He'd send in one sheet of paper: 'Dear Jay, My plan this year is to grow sales and earnings by 15 percent. Sincerely yours, Frank,'" Tom Sullivan remembered. "Jay would come in and say, 'What do I do?' I said don't change a word. Whatever the hell it is, he'll do it."[21]

Over time, the operating presidents got used to the process, and Morris and RPM slowly introduced more specific goals, with the planning reports including quarterly and even monthly revenue and profit targets, new product development, and capital spending plans. Meeting these goals did eventually become part of each president's evaluation and figured in annual bonuses.[22]

One important part of the planning process did not change, however. Although it was a negotiated process, the main input came from the operating presidents themselves, who were closest to their businesses and had the best grasp of what was possible. "We tried to push the authority and the responsibility down to the company presidents' level because we had no corporate staff," Morris said. "It was a very lean corporate staff with very good people running the individual companies."[23]

Typically, the operating company presidents received the planning form two weeks before the fall annual meeting. The presidents were asked to predict revenue for the balance of the current fiscal year, which ran until the end of May. They were also asked to estimate revenue, profit or loss, and

Wives and female relatives of corporate officers and directors and operating presidents of RPM, Inc., at the 1979 annual meeting celebrating the company's first $100 million year in sales. Peg Sullivan is shown standing third from the right.

categorical expenditures—for marketing, research, sales, general, and administration—for the next fiscal year. At the end, the presidents had two pages to describe their goals. The plans were due back by mid-February, giving Morris, Karman, and Sullivan six weeks to review them.[24]

Then, two weeks before the actual planning meetings began—usually at the end of March—Tom Sullivan and Jim Karman would sit down with Morris to offer their thoughts on the kind of targets that should be set. "No one said at the end of the day, 'When you finish the planning meetings, revenues have to be up 14 percent and earnings have to be up 18 percent.'" Morris said. "That's been the success of this company: it isn't micromanaged. I can honestly say, when any of these company presidents walked out, it was their plan."[25]

After the plan meetings, Morris put together what he called a "recap letter" to each president, setting down in writing the year's goals. Sullivan and Karman reviewed these formalized plans.[26]

Throughout the year, the presidents received a monthly report from Morris showing the previous month's results and asking for an update for the month ahead and the remainder of the fiscal year. Morris also would speak monthly, or sometimes more often, with the presidents to stay abreast of the businesses. He, in turn, would meet periodically with Karman to keep him briefed.

Several times a year, Morris also visited operating presidents on their own turf. Although there was some initial skepticism, Morris's calculated and slow approach soon won the respect of the operating company presidents. "I had a lot of company presidents call and say, 'You know, you haven't been out here for a quarter,'" he said. "'We'd like to have you come out; we want to show you some new things we're doing.'"[27]

When he did make a trip out to a plant, that cost was never charged back to the operating company, as many companies would do—for a great variety of headquarters services. "We never charged," Morris said. "There was no corporate fee. I mean when we flew out, the corporation paid the ticket."[28]

As RPM grew, Morris eventually had twenty-eight company presidents to plan with. He scheduled the planning meetings for every other day so the meetings eventually ran until early June.

Dealing with Setbacks

Obviously, no company achieves its targeted plans 100 percent of the time, year after year, so the RPM process included a safeguard known as "Plan B." Once the basic yearly plan was committed to paper, Morris and each company president would create an alternative scenario should earnings or revenue fall 10 percent short of the target for any given quarter.[29]

Because of the collaborative nature of the process, RPM's presidents weren't hesitant about kicking in Plan B if necessary. Their targets, after all, were their own. Morris recalled a time the president of Mohawk called to announce that his company wasn't going to make it and he had already initiated Plan B. "So there wasn't any yelling, screaming, and kicking," Morris said. "It was sit down and say, 'OK, we've got a problem. How are we going to work out of it? What aren't we doing that you saw when you wrote this plan?' "[30]

In the event that drastic action needed to be taken, such as plant closures or layoffs, it was up to Morris and the operating president to take any corrective measures. In all the years that Morris handled this aspect of RPM, neither Tom Sullivan nor Jim Karman ever became involved in the planning process or sat in on planning meetings.

More often than not, however, the problems were external to the operating company. RPM bought well-managed companies and retained good

managers. Because all the operating presidents were stockholders with a vested interest in RPM's success, it was exceedingly rare that an operating company president had to be replaced.

The key to keeping this system operating was trust and an open flow of information between the operating companies and RPM corporate headquarters. "The only news that killed us was the news we never heard," Morris observed. "As long as you know what's going on, you can get in with these guys. It was 'Let's sit down. We've got a problem. Let's analyze and see how to get out of it.'"[31]

The View from Outside

Over time, the RPM management style became immensely popular with the early operating presidents and was a powerful incentive for future business owners to sell to RPM. In many cases, the principal in a family business, or perhaps an heir, was ready to cash out or retire, but professional managers in the company wanted to stay. Under the RPM system, these managers, often second or third generation to the founder, could maintain control while being part of a much larger corporation. Especially in the early years, this was often a deal too good to pass up, both for managers at the acquired companies and for RPM, which benefited greatly from their expertise.

"The RPM system is geared to reward those who perform, so we have an inherent motivation to do that based on our year-end bonus and stock option pools," said Robert Senior, who joined RPM when it purchased his William Zinsser & Company in 1986. "But the pride of success is the thing that drives most of us, and it all comes from having goals and targets, committing to them in the business plan, and living up to that business plan."[32]

Clayton Bollinger, who joined RPM when it purchased Chemical Coatings, a maker of furniture stains and lacquers, observed shortly after the purchase that being with RPM "makes you set goals in formalized ways you probably wouldn't do if you were independent." On its own, the goal setting at Chemical Coatings was considerably less formal. "We never had any written plan," Bollinger said. "We just sort of naturally expected to grow an average of 10 percent to 15 percent every year. Now they want to know how you'll achieve that."[33]

Bollinger wasn't the only operating company president who appreciated RPM's formalized approach. Robert Deitz, president of Consolidated Coatings and a former employee of Frank C. Sullivan's at Acorn, joined RPM in 1989, when he arranged for the sale of Consolidated to Tom Sullivan.

"I loved the planning process," Deitz remembered. "I was learning something that I should have learned years before because it's the right way to run a business. You write your plan. You submit your plan. The executives at RPM review it. Some plans they would expand, and some they would cut back because I was too optimistic. They wanted a realistic plan, one that you would achieve, because these plans are turned in to the board of directors and used to project the company's revenue for the year."[34]

Charles G. Pauli, who joined RPM when it purchased Kop-Coat in 1990, agreed, remarking that "if we could be faulted, maybe we wait too long (to intervene)."[35]

Over the years, RPM's system proved highly effective and was praised universally for its flexibility and ability to motivate people toward the same goal. Looking back shortly after his 1999 retirement, Morris said, "I'd put our planning process up against General Motors'."[36]

Advice from the Top

At the center of this web of operating companies, RPM's corporate offices remained knowledgeable and lean. Tom Sullivan handled the acquisitions; Jim Karman dealt with the banks for financing; Jay Morris was the liaison between RPM and its operating companies. Although each of the three was adept at his function (Morris called Tom Sullivan one of the best acquisition artists in the country[37]), they continued to recognize the value of having a board of directors with vast experience.

In 1976, George F. Karch, retired chairman of the Cleveland Trust Corporation, a major

Opposite: Tom Sullivan with family members at the company's 1979 annual meeting. From left are Joan Sullivan Livingston, Sandy Sullivan, Tom, Peg Sullivan, Sue Sullivan Jacobus, and Kaki Sullivan O'Neill. Family support was critical to Tom Sullivan and RPM's success.

Above: Tom Sullivan was considered one of the best acquisition artists in the industry by the late 1970s. He had based his career on building RPM into the worldwide leader in industrial and maintenance coatings. He continued to recognize the value of having a board of directors with vast experience.

Opposite: Pictured with Tom and Jim is Bill Papenbrock, RPM's outside counsel, who played a pivotal role in the RPM acquisition program.

bank, joined the board.[38] A year later, Niles H. Hammink, retired chairman and chief executive of the Scott & Fetzer Company, a Cleveland-area manufacturer of consumer and industrial products, took a seat on the board.[39] Soon after, Les Gigax, retired president of Rubbermaid, joined the board. He was followed by Lawrence C. Jones, president and chairman of the Van Dorn Company;[40] and in 1979, Kevin O'Donnell, president of SIFCO Industries in Cleveland, was elected to the board.[41]

As CEO of a young company, Sullivan formulated a pattern of asking newly retired chairmen and CEOs of major publicly owned companies to join RPM's board, with an unwritten rule that they could stand for reelection until their 75th birthday. This gave a relatively small company the opportunity to have outstanding individuals with a great deal of expertise serve on the board. It also gave excellent board rotation, with the average tenure of a director approximately ten years. The pattern served RPM well through the 1980s and 1990s.

Meanwhile, the acquisitions continued. Early in 1977, RPM acquired Cleveland-based Tropical Industrial Coatings, a subsidiary of Grow Chemical Corporation that made industrial protective coatings. RPM merged Tropical into Republic Powdered Metals in Medina. Tropical Industrial Coatings, founded in the early 1900s, was the granddaddy of the coatings companies. Two of its salesmen, Katz and Sanders, left Tropical to form Acorn in 1906 and both employed and competed directly against Frank C. Sullivan during his Acorn and Republic years.[42]

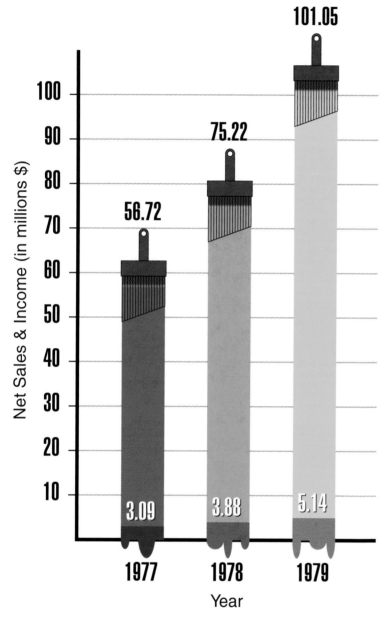

RPM's sales and earnings for 1977 through 1979. Earnings are represented by the darker area within the sales bar.

Later that same year, RPM bought the Dutch Masters Paint Company, then negotiated for the stock of Alox Corporation in Niagara Falls, New York. Alox, founded in 1926, manufactured a line of rust-preventing and corrosion-controlling products for chemical coating and lubricants makers and had a research and development laboratory in Niagara Falls. Clarence A. Weltman, Alox president, joined RPM.[43] This addition was followed by the purchase of Design/Craft Fabric Corporation of Chicago, which made fabrics such as drapes used in commercial, industrial, and residential markets.[44] Design/Craft "led us into the consumer marketplace," Karman later remarked.[45]

Before the end of 1977 and after three consecutive three-for-two stock splits, the company had a secondary underwriting of 860,000 shares, which was a combination of stocks used in acquisitions, as well as 365,000 shares from the Frank C. Sullivan estate. The issue was sold out at $10 per share.[46]

A Year of Consolidation

During 1978, RPM made only one acquisition, that of the seventy-seven-year-old Dean & Barry Company, of Columbus, Ohio. Dean & Barry was an architectural paint company that operated forty of its own retail stores, and the move was part of Sullivan's experiment with retail stores.[47]

Otherwise, 1978 was a time of consolidation and reorganization. RPM had begun to focus its attention on two areas of growth. It would continue to extend its well-established coatings into markets that had long-term growth and increase its offerings in specialized coatings.[48]

To do this, the company identified nineteen profit centers and organized them into five product lines: surface protection and maintenance; repair and restoration; hobby, recreation, and leisure; beautification; and energy.[49]

RPM's cold-process roofing products, Alumanation and Permaroof, led the surface protection line. The repair and restoration group sold Mohawk to the professional furniture repair business. The principal recreation products, Floquil–Polly S hobby and craft paints, were retail products sold by hobby shops. The beautification line included Thibaut wall coverings, Bondex surface preparation products, and the regional paints, which were marketed to retail outlets.[50] Julius Nemeth was named vice president for this group.

The reorganization was accompanied by the promotion of Jim Karman to the position of president. Tom Sullivan told shareholders at the annual meeting in September 1978 that Karman's presidency reflected Tom's decision to share more duties with his long-time friend and business partner.[51]

At the end of the decade, RPM purchased the Medina County Travel Agency from Old Phoenix National Bank. The company was renamed RPM World Travel Inc. It was very successfully managed by its president, Jim Livingston, who was able to quadruple the company's growth in revenue and in value until 1995, when Livingston retired and the company was sold.

Heading for the Eighties

In February, RPM announced the $6.2 million acquisition of Mameco International, a respected Cleveland sealants company. Founded in 1913 by Russian immigrant Isaac M. Evans—a cofounder with Katz and Sanders of the Acorn Refining Company—Mameco had annual sales of $10 million and sold the Vulkem line of urethane sealants and Monile-brand industrial, poured-in-place flooring systems.[52]

"That added to our industrial base and gave us a nice sealant company," Karman later said.[53] Within a year, RPM expanded Mameco's Cleveland plant and broke ground for a plant in Brussels, Belgium, to keep pace with the growing market for elastomeric sealants.[54] Charles M. Evans, a son of Isaac Evans, stayed on as president of the Mameco subsidiary.[55] Richard E. Klar, Mameco's treasurer, would become RPM's secretary-treasurer in 1980 and eventually team up with Jay Morris to run the corporate planning operation.[56]

At the end of the year, only three years into their five-year plan, Sullivan and Karman had good news: RPM had already reached $100 million in sales. That summer, the company threw a champagne celebration at Beaver Lodge, the training center and boardroom on RPM's grounds in Medina. As Tom Sullivan later described it, "We threw a big party for ourselves."[57]

By 1980, RPM had already exceeded $100 million in sales, driven forward by acquisitions, but it needed to be reorganized.

CHAPTER FIVE

THE LEARNING PROCESS DOES NOT STOP

1980–1984

I liked [RPM stock] from the beginning. It's a steady stock, a stock to hold.

—Ruth Huston, Beardstown Ladies Investment Club

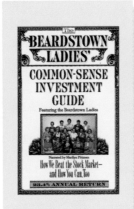

BY REACHING $100 MILLION IN sales two years ahead of its timetable, RPM exceeded even Tom Sullivan's and Jim Karman's most hopeful predictions. But this rapid growth came with a risk. Only a few days after RPM's "great big party," three directors showed up at the company's Georgian headquarters building and confronted Tom Sullivan.

The message was simple and brought us back to reality quickly. Essentially, they said that we were building a house of cards that would fall around us if certain actions were not taken. At the time, we had twenty-one operating companies, and it was George Karch who told us we had to get rid of those operations that no longer suited our financial criteria. Les Gigax indicated that although we had corporate planning, there was no strong annual plan at the operating level, which was necessary to ensure internal growth, . . . and Niles Hammink informed me we had a bunch of entrepreneurs running around with only their own interests in mind and not those of RPM.[1]

Eight years of rapid growth had created a hodgepodge. It was time, the trio told Sullivan, to look over his portfolio, pick the winners, and sell off the rest.[2]

The National Economy Stumbles

This challenge was complicated by the state of the U.S. economy. After limping through most of the 1970s, the domestic economy took a sharp downturn. High oil costs, rising interest rates, and high unemployment undercut industrial and consumer growth. This turmoil overseas helped propel Ronald Reagan into office in 1980. As Sullivan and Karman said in their joint message to shareholders in that year's annual report, "At the time this letter is being written to you, we are in the low point of what has been characterized as a severe recession. In fact, for the first time in many years, the first quarter of our fiscal year, 1981, will be relatively equal to the first quarter of last year."[3] In the summer, traditionally RPM's best period, sales actually dropped 4 percent, leading Sullivan to observe that RPM would be "playing catch-up ball" for the rest of the year.[4]

Nevertheless, Sullivan and Karman moved quickly on their directors' sound advice. The corporate planning function was bolstered, and cash management and cost control programs were initiated.[5] They next looked over their portfolio of companies with an eye toward keeping only specialty coating or maintenance businesses that were unaffected by the economy. These retained businesses also had to have gross margins of 40 percent or more, with potential operating margins of 15 percent or more, the financial characteristic that delineates the difference between commodity and niche markets. As a result of these criteria, $400 million in assets would be divested over the next several years, notably the regional architectural businesses: Briggs Bros., Dutch Masters, Mac-O-Lac, F. O. Pierce, and Dean & Barry.

"These operations weren't producing in proportion to overall effort," Sullivan later told a reporter.[6]

Growth from the Inside

This period of regrouping, which would last until the mid-1980s, marks the slowest period in RPM's history of acquisitions. Between 1980 and 1984, RPM negotiated only four acquisitions, totaling less than $30 million. Instead, much of the time was spent focusing on growing current RPM businesses and developing internal opportunities.

Mameco broke ground for a new plant in Belgium to expand production of its urethane elastomer roof sealers.[7] The company projected that the market for Mameco's urethane sealants would grow from $590 million in 1979 to $1.6 billion in 1985.[8]

Providing Cover

Gates Engineering began a major push into the single-ply sheet-roofing market—an area that Sullivan and Karman said they considered "RPM's strongest growth opportunity in the immediate future."[9] In 1980, Gates added fifty thousand square feet to its Wilmington, Delaware, plant.[10] RPM predicted that within five years Gates's business could quadruple, from $12 million to almost $50 million annually.[11] Analysts said RPM held about 8 percent of the $120 million single-ply roofing market.[12]

Gates's single-ply roofing sheets were relatively new products and were making inroads into the traditional "built up" commercial roofing as an economical and durable way to create a waterproof surface. Most builders still covered roofs with several layers of asphalt-filled sheets of felt joined together at the seams with tar. This was a labor-intensive process, but when asphalt was cheap, it was still economical. The rapid rise in oil prices, however, coupled with the improved single-ply products, had tipped the scales in favor of sheet roofing.[13]

RPM's judgment was quickly proven correct. The market grew so rapidly that even after the plant expansion, Gates was running at capacity. At that point, Gates turned to Haartz-Mason of Boston to produce sheet roofing on contract at its Watertown, Massachusetts, plant.

"Gates liked Haartz-Mason's expertise in manufacturing," Sullivan told a trade publication. Before long, he was negotiating RPM's acquisition of Haartz-Mason. The deal was completed later in 1980, with RPM purchasing all outstanding shares of Haartz-Mason stock for $4.05 million.[14] The Watertown plant was quickly expanded, first doubling and then tripling capacity.[15]

Haartz-Mason was a fifty-four-year-old, privately held company with annual sales of $8 million when RPM bought it. In addition to single-ply roofing, the company made a range of other synthetic products including flow-control diaphragms with automotive applications and wrappings for power cables.[16] In typical RPM acquisition fashion, existing management, including the general manager, would stay on. RPM announced that it intended to retain and expand the new subsidiary's existing product line.[17]

With Haartz-Mason providing low-end products and Gates covering the midprice range, RPM moved to cover the premium end through a joint venture with a German company, Braas GmbH. Republic Powdered Metals (now a subsidiary of RPM, Inc.) had been U.S. marketing agent for Braas's product line for two years. The new business would be a partnership and was called AGR. Its $4 million, forty-thousand-square-foot factory was built in Charlotte, North Carolina, and opened in the fall of 1982. "To get involved in the manufacture of PIB is easier said than done," Sullivan told *Rubber & Plastics News*. "Theirs is a proven technology, and it's a good product."[18]

Rolling On

Considering the state of the economy, 1980 and 1981 weren't bad years for RPM. Its earnings grew at 11 percent. But RPM's shareholders were used to earnings growth that was closer to 20 percent annually, and it was a relieved Tom Sullivan who announced in late 1981, "We are confident that this year we are well on our way to our thirty-fifth consecutive year of earnings growth, at a rate more along our traditional lines."

Analysts tended to agree. One analyst, familiar with the recession-resistant nature of many of the company's products and confident of its ability to rebound, asked a reporter rhetorically, "How long can you live with a leaking roof?"[19]

The Talsol Acquisition

Sullivan was right: RPM's numbers picked up again and its businesses settled down. Once again Tom Sullivan was looking for good acquisitions. In the summer of 1983—after almost two years without buying a single company—he once again announced a deal. This time, RPM had negotiated the purchase of the Talsol Corporation for $5.5 million.

The Talsol deal actually began in 1980, when an executive of Talsol's ad agency mentioned the company to Jerry Siebert of Siebert Associates, a mergers and acquisitions firm that specialized in brokering the sale of paint companies. Siebert had already found several acquisitions for RPM, and the Siebert broker approached David T. Stebbins, Talsol's owner, on RPM's behalf. "No way am I going to sell this company," Stebbins thought to himself, and responded by seeking a high price and a cash deal. RPM countered with a lower-priced offer in stock.[20]

Over the months, the two sides went back and forth. "RPM kept offering 'X,' and I kept saying no," Stebbins later told Business Week magazine. "Then the day before what was supposed to be one last meeting, I was having breakfast on my back porch, and it struck me that I was coming up on sixty years old and I might be foolish to turn them down. RPM had more than thirty straight years of sales and earnings increases, their management was sharp, and their stock was very salable. On the spot, I decided to ask for 10 percent more, making the deal $5.5 million in RPM stock, and I got it."[21]

In return, RPM got a company that made touch-up paints and other products for auto repair shops and shade-tree mechanics—most sold under the Mar-Hyde brand name—with annual sales of $6.5 million.[22] "With the acquisition of Talsol in July 1983, we are starting to replace the low margin sales that we've spun off with operations of high margin sales, and I think you can expect more of this," Sullivan told a reporter from the hometown Medina County Gazette.[23]

The Picture Brightens

By the end of 1983, as the Talsol deal was closing, the U.S. economy had indeed pulled out of its slump. Throughout the recession of the early 1980s, like the recession of the early 1970s, RPM had continued its streak of increased earnings and revenues. In 1983, the company was selected by Dun's Business Month magazine as a "Dividend Achiever." The magazine noted that RPM's dividend growth had averaged a compounded rate of 41.2 percent for the previous decade. After compensating for stock splits, the RPM dividend rose to 56 cents a share.[24]

With the economy poised to boom throughout the rest of the 1980s, RPM continued to earn the admiration of investment groups. In late 1984, Shirley Gross, a member of the famous Beardstown Ladies Investment Club's Stock Selection Committee, came across RPM in the Value Line investment guide. She recommended the stock to the one-year-old group, which initially purchased thirty-five shares and then increased its holdings to one hundred shares. In ten years, those one hundred shares produced a 271 percent return, and RPM was one of the group's largest holdings.[25]

The Testors product line included model paints and plastic models. Testors was an early consumer-oriented acquisition and had deep brand loyalty in its niche market.

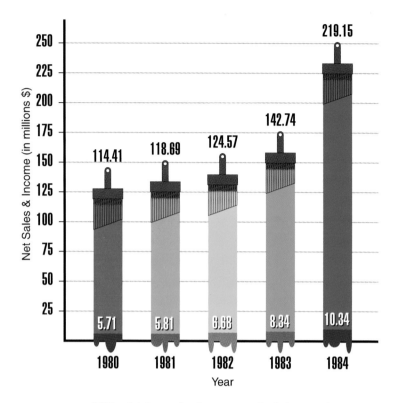

"I liked it from the beginning," club member Ruth Huston said in the group's best-selling 1994 investment guide. "It's a steady stock, a stock to hold."

Testors Corporation

Within months of the Talsol purchase, RPM announced another significant consumer acquisition. Sullivan and Karman had negotiated the purchase of Testors Corporation, a well-known Illinois-based company that made glue and paints for model builders. Testors had been owned by Jupiter Industries, of Chicago,[26] and had annual sales of $17 million and one hundred employees. Testors President Charles G. Miller would stay on to run the operation.[27]

Testors was the creation of two Swedes, Axel Karlson and Nils F. Testor. Karlson had developed a nitrocellulose cement that was first used in 1929 to repair women's stockings. Karlson's company struggled, and a few years later he sold it to Testor. In 1936, the company introduced its cement for model building.[28]

RPM saw Testors as a company with a leadership position in its key products in a market—the hobby sector—that had strong growth potential. The company was already in that sector with its Floquil-Polly S line of hobby and craft products.[29]

Euclid Chemical Company

In August, after courting its owner, Lawrence Korach, for more than five years, RPM acquired a company in its backyard: Euclid Chemical Company, a seventy-four-year-old Cleveland firm that produced concrete additives.[30] In addition to its concrete products, which included chemicals that allowed builders to pour concrete in cold weather, Euclid Chemical manufactured and sold masonry and waterproofing products and grouting materials.[31]

Owned by the Korach family, the company had been founded in 1910 and stayed a private, family-run business. When RPM approached Euclid, it was owned by the sixty-eight-year-old Korach, who had purchased 50 percent of the company from his cousin in 1946, then bought the company outright by 1951. He was joined in business by two sons, including Jeffrey Korach. His brother Ken eventually left the family business to be a teacher, and later returned to run it as part of RPM.

"We grew the business slowly," Jeff Korach remembered. "By the time 1984 came, when we were acquired by RPM, we were doing about $12 million worth of business a year. At the time, RPM was buying smaller family businesses, and they were about $120 million a year. I thought they were the biggest company I ever saw, being a public company and so forth."[32]

Lawrence Korach officially retired after the acquisition, but Jeff signed a three-year agreement to stay and run Euclid as a subsidiary of RPM.[33] The relationship ended up being extended into 2000, when Jeff Korach took over a major RPM business.

Frank's Early Start

Naturally, Tom had wanted his children to be a part of the family company, and most of them began working for RPM in high school, learning about hard work and leadership. When Frank was just seventeen years old and working in an RPM plant during the summer break, he took in one of his father's early lessons.

Frank Sullivan joined RPM in 1987 after first working in banking and finance. Like his father and grandfather, Frank attended Culver Military Academy, but he pursued his university education at the University of North Carolina as a Morehead Scholar.

"When pallets came in, they had these big cardboard caps on them, and one guy, I forget his name, had stacked up a bunch of these and made a little hammock, and the guys would take turns taking naps," Frank said.

I wasn't tattling or anything, but at some point I told my father about it. He picked up the phone to call the plant manager, and I said, "What are you doing?" He said, "Well, I'm going to fire these guys." I thought about it and said, "You can't do that." He hung up the phone and said, "What do you mean I can't do that?" I said, "I'll never be able to walk into that place again." He said, "Well, you know, you better be smarter about what you tell me. If it's important, you let me know. If it's being one of the guys over there, you'd better figure out the difference."[34]

But working at RPM during the summers was a far cry from joining the company as a life-long career, and Frank had a series of personal ambitions. Like his father, Frank attended Culver Military Academy, where he was named personnel cadet officer. But after graduating, he took a semester off for an Outward Bound course in the mountains, then was awarded a Morehead scholarship to the University of North Carolina. There, besides excelling in academics and fencing, Frank Sullivan "had some really neat opportunities for intern programs in public service and on Wall Street during the summers." Frank's biggest opportunity at North Carolina came in the form of one Barbara O'Rourke from Greensboro, North Carolina, whom he met during his junior year at school and subsequently married in 1984.

"So I didn't go to work at RPM," Frank said. "When I got out of school, I went into the banking business. I had a real desire to come back and work for RPM and my father at some point, but I wanted to create some of my own success and really learn something that I could bring back."[35]

With a new joint venture, however, Tom Sullivan found his opening to lure Frank to RPM.

"We were living in Chicago, and I just wasn't ready," Frank said. "But he's a consummate salesman. After I'd worked four years in the banking business, he took us out to dinner, my wife and I, and she's one of ten kids from North Carolina. He mentioned that they had formed this joint venture with a German firm, and they had just opened a plant in Charlotte, North Carolina, and they were looking for regional sales managers, and if I knew anybody that was interested, let him know. My wife and I went back to our apartment, and that was it. We were going to North Carolina."[36]

But when Frank did come to work for RPM, his mother remembered him saying, "Dad, this is something I've always wanted to do, be a part of RPM. But I want this understood up front. I'll give it five years; you give it five years. But if for whatever reason, either my side or your side, it doesn't work, I want to be able to walk away from here with no bad feelings."[37]

The relationship worked, however, and before long, Frank Sullivan was promoted to vice president of corporate development.

Zinsser's Bulls Eye sealer was introduced in the early 1980s as the first effective "whole house" water-based primer sealer. This product was one of Zinsser's most successful offerings.

CHAPTER SIX

THE TRANSFORMATION BEGINS

1985–1989

Someday, you're going to get rid of this company. When you do, I want to be on top of your list.

—Tom Sullivan,
to the Sun board of directors
regarding Carboline in 1979

RPM KICKED OFF 1985 WITH confidence. "During the recession of the early 1980s, while many companies were experiencing depressed sales and earnings, RPM aggressively positioned itself for the future," Tom Sullivan declared in the 1985 annual report. To *Investor's Business Daily* he said, "I do not see our growth rate slowing down. RPM is positioning itself to do some aggressive things in the future."[1]

These bold predictions were made despite Wall Street's unease with RPM's debt-to-equity ratio. The two late 1984 acquisitions—Euclid and Testors, totaling $20 million—were made possible by issuing debt, which raised concerns that the company was overextended.[2] Sullivan, however, remained unfazed.

It wouldn't take long for RPM to live up to his words. In January 1985, RPM announced it had purchased Westfield Coatings of Westfield, Massachusetts, for about $11 million. Westfield made coatings for packaging and textiles. The company had been founded in 1953 and had sales of about $6 million annually, mostly in the northeastern United States.[3]

Exiting Part of the Roofing Business

This was the only acquisition for 1985; RPM spent much of the year waging a price war with

Firestone Tire & Rubber. After a couple of successful years in the single-ply roof-sheeting business, market competitor Firestone touched off a pricing competition. Instead of rolling in the dirt on price, Sullivan and Karman began to rethink RPM's role in the market for single-ply roofing. Not only was it outside RPM's traditional competencies in coatings, but the product was rapidly turning from a high-margin specialty item to a low-margin commodity.[4] Firestone had entered the market late but aggressively sold its products on price, eventually reducing the price from 60 cents a square foot to 17 cents a square foot.[5]

By 1987, after two consecutive years of operating losses in the business, RPM had had enough. That year, Gates Engineering's roof-sheeting line was divested, leading Sullivan to remark that "we have no business being in rubber products competition with Firestone."[6] It was an experience that further reinforced the company's belief in focusing on niche markets and avoiding commodity where price, instead of people and service, makes the difference.

Zinsser's DIF wallpaper stripper. Purchased in 1986, Zinsser brought 150 years of experience to RPM and an established portfolio of products, including its Bulls Eye primer.

The setback, however, was confined to only one particular business within Gates. RPM's other operating companies, including many of the new ones like Talsol, Testors, and Euclid, were growing quickly. Testors, for example, regularly posted a 15 percent growth rate through the mid-1980s.[7]

By the end of fiscal May 31, 1985, RPM had maintained its "very enviable record as a publicly-owned company," Sullivan said.

During the first half of the 1980s, we reinvested approximately 40 percent of our pretax income into expansion of our plant and equipment; we eliminated $20 million of marginal product line sales; and added, at the same time, through acquisition, four new marketing lines in our basic consumer/do-it-yourself and industrial areas, which will bring growth with strong operating earnings.[8]

Carboline Company

The momentum would spill into the next year. In August 1985, Sullivan announced RPM's largest acquisition to that date, a $60 million deal for Carboline Company.[9] With sales of $65 million, Carboline made specialty chemical and corrosion coatings for bridges, highways, and offshore structures, and coatings to protect structures from high temperatures. The company was headquartered in St. Louis and had plants in Fremont, California; Green Bay, Wisconsin; Lake Charles, Louisiana; and Xenia, Ohio.

Carboline was a strategic acquisition that Tom Sullivan had been pursuing since 1971. In 1979, he had tried to buy the company from its founder Stanley L. Lopata but lost out to a higher bid from Sun Oil. Like many of its peers, the giant oil company was diversifying into the petrochemical business. For Sullivan, though, it stung to lose the acquisition.

TESTORS' BEST-SELLING "SECRET" TOPS 800,000

THE TESTORS UNIT POPPED UP ON SOME top secret radar when, in July 1986, it released a new model airplane which it called the "F-19 Stealth" fighter.

Soon, U.S. Representative Ronald Wyden of Oregon was waving the F-19 in front of television cameras and wondering how a model company's chief designer, John Andrews, could so accurately produce a replica of a top-secret aircraft under development at Lockheed.

Neither the aerospace company nor the government ever commented on the accuracy of the model. Andrews would say only that he put together the model, which he believed to be "80 percent accurate," from scraps of information he picked up from friends in the Southern California aerospace industry. "He did a very clever thing," said a Lockheed spokesperson. "[I]f there is a stealth fighter, most of the secrets are probably inside the plane anyway."[1]

A few years later, when the Air Force unveiled its real Stealth fighter, the F-117A, the model and the real Stealth were no twins. When the *Wall Street Journal* came calling this time, Andrews pointed out that he never claimed to have nailed the actual design. And Testors spokesman John Dewey told the *Journal* that "Anyone who has two eyes can see the resemblance is fleeting at best" and that if the F-19 model had been more accurate, "there'd have been guys with trench coats all over us." In the meantime, Testors sold 800,000 F-19s at about $10 each, which made its plane the top-selling model of all time by a wide margin.[2]

He talked about it with Lopata at the time, asking, "'Stanley, how could you do this to me?' Lopata said, 'Tom, you don't have $50 million you can give me, do you?' The answer was, 'No, I don't.'"

But RPM was clearly a better match for Carboline than Sun, and Sullivan had no intention of forgetting about the company. After Sun closed the acquisition, Sullivan wrote a letter to its CEO and declared, "Someday, you're going to get rid of this company. When you do, I want to be on top of your list."[10]

Sullivan was right. As a rule, the oil businesses didn't fare very well in specialty and petrochemical industries, and by the 1980s they began to divest these units. Carboline, under Sun, had experienced increases in sales but decreases in earnings while dramatically increasing its corporate and sales staffs. By 1985, Sun management had decided to divest it. Mike Tellor, who joined Carboline in 1972, was in upper management when Sun's board reached its decision.

"They came to us and said, 'We're going to go ahead and sell it,' and they went through a formal procedure," Tellor remembered. "It was like an auction. They were going to send out a prospectus to about a hundred companies, then whittle that down to ten. In the summer of 1985, these ten companies came to Carboline. One of them was RPM."[11]

RPM had known from Carboline personnel of the pending sale of the company but agreed to do nothing until it was announced officially. Jim Karman spotted an article in the *Wall Street Journal* mentioning that Sun had hired Lehman Brothers to help sell Carboline, and he called Sullivan, who was at a sales meeting in Orlando. Sullivan recalled what happened next.

On Monday morning, I called John Herrmann [of Lehman Brothers] from Orlando and said, "I'm going to be in your office tomorrow (in) New

York." He said, "There's no need for that." I said, "Yeah, there's a great need for it.... I want to make sure you know who we are." He said, "Well, I've not heard of you before." I said, "I'm going to be there."[12]

After meeting with Herrmann, Sullivan returned to Medina and met with RPM board member Donald K. Miller, an investment banker then with Blyth Eastman Paine Webber. With competition from several global companies, Miller advised him that the best way to win Carboline was to preempt Sun's auction. Sullivan needed to make his best offer before the auction began and stipulate that the offer was good for only one day. If the offer was declined, RPM wouldn't participate in the auction, thereby preventing Sun from using the RPM offer as a starting point or as a fallback should the auction fail to produce a higher price.[13]

In July, Sullivan returned to New York to meet again with Herrmann and a group of Lehman Brothers executives. Sullivan explained how RPM would buy Carboline, most likely financing the deal through a stock offering after the purchase to keep its debt in line.

Then something happened that rattled Sullivan a bit.

Halfway through this presentation, in comes this old, scruffy guy with a shoeshine kit. Herrmann looks at me and says, "Tom, you want your shoes shined?" I'm floored. I say OK. Herrmann says, "Sit up on my desk." So I'm sitting on his desk, my feet hanging over, this guy shining my shoes, and Herrmann says, "Continue with your presentation." And I did. I was flustered, but I finished it and they let us go ahead.[14]

After that meeting, the investment bankers set up a meeting just before Labor Day between Sullivan and the Sun executive handling the sale. At their hotel before the meeting, Sullivan, Karman, and Miller rehearsed their presentation. Remembering how the surprise entrance of the shoeshiner had disrupted Sullivan, Miller said, "Tom, they will do everything they can to throw your presentation off; that's just the game people play because if they fluster you, it puts them up a little bit.... But today you play hardball."[15]

When they arrived at the Boston office in their coats and ties, they were met by Herrmann and Sun executive Bruce Lindsay, who, by their dress, had just come from the golf course. As they sat down and Sullivan began to make his pitch, there was a knock on the door. A woman entered with hamburgers, french fries, and soft drinks. Herrmann looked at Sullivan and said, "We haven't eaten yet. Is it OK if we eat while you give your presentation?"

"Eat," Sullivan said, "and I'll give my presentation afterwards."[16]

Sullivan finally presented an offer of $60 million to a cool reception. The bankers thanked the trio for coming, and the RPM team headed for the elevator. But Herrmann followed and asked them to come back to continue negotiations; Sun wanted another $5 million.

Sullivan wasn't negotiating. Over the next three hours, the selling team excused themselves several times for private huddles before coming back with demands that dropped to $62 million, then $61 million. But Sullivan stood firm at $60 million. "Then John Herrmann came back and sat down and said, 'Congratulations. I don't know how you did it, but you nailed it.'"[17]

While the Lehman Brothers team had gamesmanship on its side, Sullivan had an ace up his sleeve, too. During their due diligence, RPM's lawyers had come across a contract Sun had signed with its Carboline managers that gave the managers a bonus for any deal they signed more than $55 million. "We knew where their floor was," said Sullivan. "So then it was just a question as to how much we had to go to get to a preemptive bid, and Sun's board said, 'If they hit $60 million, take it.'"[18]

In October, Sullivan told his shareholders that while RPM expected to incur some costs putting Carboline back in shape, the purchase would eventually increase company sales by 43 percent. In 1985, RPM had adjusted sales of $289.8 million, an increase of 26.5 percent over the year before and its first $200 million year.[19]

First, however, RPM needed to take some uncharacteristic action. When RPM bought the company, Mike Tellor was Carboline's vice president of international and experienced the upheaval. "There was a lot of activity going on at the time because it was a pretty risky acquisition," Tellor recalled. "It was risky because it was a very large acquisition for RPM. Carboline had been a very, very profitable company through the late 1970s, but in the early 1980s, things didn't go so well. The basic market sort of disappeared, and the overhead went way up."[20]

The first thing necessary was to trim Carboline's bloated headcount, which resulted in Tellor's rapid promotion to executive vice president. All told, about one hundred people, or 20 percent of the total workforce, were let go almost immediately.[21] In the end, Sullivan was right: Carboline, under newly installed president Bud Steinberg, who had previously been Carboline's executive vice president but left after Sun took over, went on to exceed analysts' expectations.

"Coming out of Sun, we had gotten a lot of training and were quite good at writing these gigantic, five-year plans that you'd spend all year writing. It was big-company thinking, and there

was very little value that came out of it," Tellor said. "When we joined RPM and were introduced to the RPM planning process, I viewed that as more targeted, constructive, and usable. It helped Carboline quite a bit."[22]

Paying for Carboline

In the short run, however, RPM had exposed itself to considerable risk. To buy Carboline, RPM had to borrow $60 million from National City Bank of Cleveland, an amount which was equal to its net worth at the time. With so much debt, Sullivan and Karman would have to keep out of the acquisitions market for a while. But with the market continuing to consolidate, they were in no mood to wait. Sullivan announced at the annual meeting that the company was planning a secondary stock offering of two million shares, which he hoped would raise $30 million.

"Although Carboline can cover all of its expenses on its own, in the next six months we want to put the balance sheet back into shape so we can continue with acquisitions," Sullivan said, adding that RPM would reduce debt by selling

At the 1987 annual meeting, Tom Sullivan proudly announced that the company had a forty-year streak of consecutive record sales, earnings, and earnings per share.

some assets.[23] Within less than a month, the company divested itself of Dean & Barry.

By the end of 1986, RPM could show the benefits of the Carboline acquisition. Sales that year stood at $338.85 million. Earnings rose from $13 million to $16.74 million. But earnings per share, diluted by the new offering, were up only 1.9 percent, from $1.03 to $1.05.

"Carboline operations did not contribute to our 1986 earnings in any meaningful way," Sullivan said. "However, the company did absorb all costs of the acquisition and extensive reorganization. We fully expect strong contribution from Carboline in our 1987 fiscal year."[24]

The Acquisitions Continue: The Zinsser Story

To Sullivan, the stock offering was worthwhile because it enabled RPM to remain in the acquisitions market. Almost immediately afterward, he announced the acquisition of PCI Industries for two hundred thousand shares of RPM. He had been pursuing the Riviera Beach, Florida, company for seven years.[25]

PCI had annual sales of $6 million. The company sold a line of adhesives, sealants, and other specialty coatings for the DIY market. Company president Anthony J. Rose and his management team planned to continue running the company.[26] "There's very little interference," he told the *Wall Street Journal* four years later. "Four years after buying my company, it's been just as they said."[27]

More acquisitions followed with alacrity near the end of 1986. In December, RPM announced it had purchased American Emulsions, coming out of Dalton, Georgia. American Emulsions had $10 million in annual sales and offered a line of coatings and chemicals used in the textile, carpet, and paper industries. The company's management team, led by President Charles Cofield, stayed on with RPM.[28]

Far more significant was the purchase of William Zinsser & Company of Somerset, New Jersey. Zinsser, with $23 million in annual sales, was a leader in the do-it-yourself market for shellac, primers and sealers, and wallpaper-removing chemicals.[29] It had been an institution in the shellac business since its founding by German immigrant William Zinsser in 1849.[30] His company was the first to manufacture bleached shellac in the United States.[31]

Two years after World War II ended, Zinsser introduced Bulls-I-Namel, now known as B-I-N, the original white-pigmented, shellac-based primer-sealer. The revolutionary product combined three functions: priming, sealing, and stain killing.[32] In 1947, a fourth-generation Zinsser took the helm: Edward Walworth Jr., son-in-law of William Zinsser III, was selected by the William and Rudolph Zinsser families. Walworth was soon joined by Gardner R. Cunningham. The two headed the company until 1985, when Bob Senior became president.[33]

The 1980s proved to be a period of development for Zinsser, and several new products were introduced. The company's Bulls Eye 1-2-3 debuted as the first effective water-based primer-sealer. Soon, SHIELDZ Universal Wallcovering Primer was introduced as the first white-pigmented, fast-drying, one-step wall preparation. In 1985, Zinsser Cover-Stain was introduced as the first fast-drying

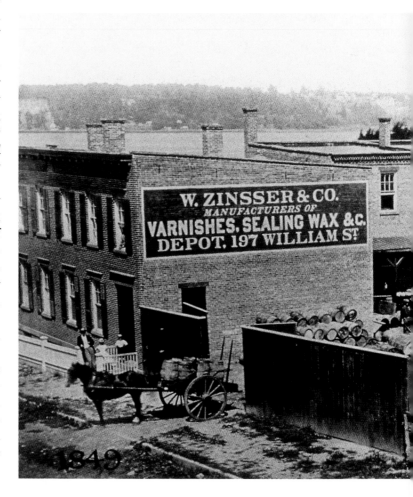

whole house oil-based primer-sealer. The patented PaperTiger Scoring Tool for wallpaper removal was launched in the same year.[34]

Zinsser had been family owned and run for 137 years. But Walworth retired by the mid-1980s, meaning that no member of the Zinsser family was involved in the day-to-day operations. Before long, Cunningham and Senior began soliciting bids for the company.[35]

"RPM had Zinsser in its sights many, many years ago, mostly because Zinsser has always had a reputation for high-quality shellac products," Senior said. "Mr. Gardner Cunningham was known to Tom Sullivan, and he's a very personable, warm human being. He asked a number of questions, but his concentration was making sure that the people who reported to me were happy, that I was happy, and that I felt needed and comfortable."[36]

During the negotiations, RPM emerged at the top of the list of potential acquiring companies. "I

Above: Because of its easy application and effectiveness, Bulls Eye 1-2-3 had strong sales among consumers. The product continued to thrive as an RPM brand.

Left: Zinsser was far older than RPM. Pictured in 1849, the company produced high-quality shellac and became the industry leader in primer sealers.

think RPM had the inside track psychologically because there was a comfort there," Senior said. "The RPM routine was comforting for everybody because Cunningham didn't want someone that was going to buy the company and just cannibalize it and destroy it."[37]

The prestigious New York investment firm, Dillon, Read & Company, was hired to run the auction process for the Zinsser Company. In his usual fashion, Sullivan found a way to preempt the auction process, offering the price that he thought was best for both buyer and seller. If the price and conditions were not accepted, he would move out of the auction process. Don Miller and Jim Karman were at the pricing meeting, and when the price was rejected, the three left the meeting, indicating they would be back at their hotel and would be leaving New York on a 4 P.M. plane.

The broker immediately shot back, "Get an earlier one."

But the story would not end so easily. Jim Karman recalled, "On the way back to the hotel, I remember Don Miller saying, 'I think we lost this one, Tom.' Then we were having lunch in Tom's room when the phone rang. Tom answered it and looked back at us smiling and saying, 'They want to know if Senior will get a contract.'"[38]

In the years ahead, RPM would use this pre-emptive method with a great deal of success in auctions. The majority of those that were not successful generally ended in sales at a lower price or broke an auction that would come back on the market at a later time.

After the acquisition was completed, Cunningham retired and Senior remained president of the company.

Environmental Awareness

Since the early 1970s, when Tom Sullivan decided to create RPM as a holding company, the entire paint industry had been grappling with a variety of concerns about the environmental hazards of paint and paint making.[39]

In the 1970s, the federal government began to pass a series of laws to reduce air pollution, beginning with the Clean Air Act of 1970. That act's main target was the reduction of auto emissions. Later amendments would target the release into the atmosphere of chlorofluorocarbons (CFCs), which were used as propellants in aerosol cans, and volatile organic compounds (VOCs).[40] Alternatives were found for CFCs, and the industry has continued to find alternatives to VOCs, notably the use of water-thinned polymer paints and paints with a high-solid, low-solvent composition. The Clean Air Act of 1990 tightened the laws limiting the release of VOCs.[41]

In June 1986, Sullivan told the *Wall Street Transcript* about the challenges of creating environmentally sound products.

We have to stay on top of that continually. Externally, it becomes an opportunity because there's a lot of very good companies in our industry that are

Purchased for $60 million, Carboline was a transformative acquisition for RPM, and a valuable one. Its products were used all over the world, including this bridge in Korea.

of smaller size that are seeing the same challenges in their own operations, and don't have quite the R&D and capital necessary to meet those challenges.[42]

The transition from solvent-based formulations was particularly an issue for some of RPM's industrial product lines, Sullivan told the financial weekly.[43]

Closing Out the Eighties

With Carboline and Zinsser aboard, RPM spent 1987 once again adjusting to the new companies, paying down its debt load, and, as always, scouting for new opportunities. At the end of the fiscal year, Tom Sullivan told a reporter for the *Wall Street*

Transcript, "The last year and a half or two years have been an important time in our history." Indeed, 1987 marked RPM's fortieth consecutive record year in sales, earnings, and earnings per share.

In the *Wall Street Transcript* article, Sullivan noted that the company had broadened its acquisitions horizon to include specialty chemical companies; increased its market share in corrosion and waterproofing products through Carboline; and divested itself of $60 million in product lines that had become unprofitable, including the single-ply roofing market.

"Eighty percent of our volume comes from products that ... either waterproof or rustproof existing structures throughout the industrial world," Sullivan said. "We see increasing market share in the corrosion areas and in waterproofing. They're huge markets and nobody has a significant percentage of any of those markets."[44]

Later that year, Sullivan also announced that RPM had reached an agreement to acquire

Craft House Corporation of Toledo, Ohio. Craft House, with annual sales of $20 million, sold a broad line of hobby products, including the famous Paint-by-Numbers art kits.[45] The deal to buy Craft House was a stock swap valued at about $25.3 million.

Craft House had been founded in 1950 when Detroit graphic artist Dan Robbins, borrowing from a technique of Leonardo da Vinci, came up with a diagram on a canvas board that allowed anyone to create a painting. "I remembered reading about how Leonardo would challenge his apprentices by handing out numbered patterns indicating where certain colors should be used," Robbins told a reporter when the Detroit Historical Museum opened a Paint-by-Numbers exhibit. "I thought it was a great idea that could be adapted for novices who want to make their own paintings." The first design was called "The Painter." The kits, which included paints and brushes, sold for $2.50 each. In four years, $80 million in kits had been sold.[46] The company later expanded into other craft and hobby products, including a PC-based fashion design program for Barbie dolls.[47]

This acquisition was followed by the 1988 purchase of Chemical Specialties, of Baltimore, for $5.7 million. The company's CHEMSPEC line of coatings and cleaners for the textile industry sold nationwide. Founders Robert G. Hughes and Daniel F. Savanuck, president and vice chairman, respectively, continued to lead Chemical Specialties.[48]

Heading into the next year, RPM bid farewell to two longtime employees. Julius Nemeth and Bob Fleming, both of whom had worked with Frank C. Sullivan at Acorn.

Board member Niles Hammink, former chairman and CEO of Scott & Fetzer Company, died that year. His seat on the board was filled by Stephen Stranahan, the former chairman of Craft House.

Meanwhile, the company's senior management continued to earn the respect of the financial press. Sullivan joined the ranks of America's greatest corporate leaders when *Financial World* magazine awarded him a bronze medal in the "CEO of the Decade" awards. The publication gave Jack Welch of General Electric its gold medal. Sullivan's fellow bronze-medal winners included Michael Eisner of the Walt Disney Company, Bill Gates of Microsoft, and Roberto C. Goizueta of Coca-Cola.[49]

Before fiscal 1989 ended, RPM had acquired three more companies. The first was Label Systems of Bridgeport, Connecticut, a $7 million processor of specialized coatings and adhesives marketed to the printing and labeling industries. This was followed by the purchase of Lindbergh Hobbies for $2.125 million.

The third acquisition was Consolidated Coatings Corporation, a Cleveland firm with a long history of working with RPM and the Sullivan family. Robert Deitz, who was Consolidated's top executive when it was sold, had worked for Frank Sullivan at Acorn Refining in the late 1940s and spent almost two decades in Tom Sullivan's sights after he lured away one of Sullivan's top sales people.

"Tom called me and said, 'I understand that you've recruited one of my men in Michigan. You shouldn't do that,'" Deitz recalled.

After Deitz suggested the two men meet face-to-face to discuss the matter, Sullivan drove to Deitz's downtown Cleveland office, intending to share a piece of his mind. Deitz listened calmly to what Sullivan had to say, and then Deitz said, "Tom, I'd like to ask you two questions. First, did the sales rep have a noncompete clause in his contract?"

No, Sullivan said.

"And my second question: Did I in any way say anything derogatory about your fine company?" Sullivan agreed that nothing negative had been said.

Zinsser's wallpaper stripping product rolls down the assembly line. By concentrating on buying into smaller, niche markets, RPM expanded throughout the entire coatings industry.

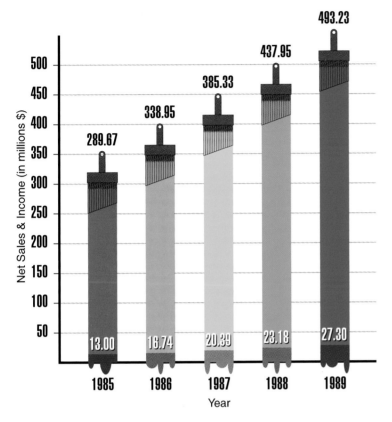

RPM's sales and earnings for 1985 through 1989. Earnings are represented by the darker area within the sales bar.

Sullivan was still interested if Deitz ever changed his mind. More than twenty years and twenty boxes of chocolate later, Deitz called Sullivan and said, "Tom, we're ready. Are you ready?"[50]

On September 15, 1989, Consolidated became a wholly owned subsidiary of RPM. True to RPM's classic acquisition model, Deitz stayed on as a valuable RPM contributor until his retirement twelve years later.

These new companies helped push sales that year to $493.23 million, RPM's forty-second consecutive record year. Heading into the 1990s, RPM boasted one of the industry's strongest intellectual teams of experienced managers.

"The reasons behind RPM's success are fourfold," Sullivan and Karman wrote.

First, we basically serve noncyclical markets. Further, our internal planning process is vigorous and assures that even the smallest of our business units receives the management expertise of a much larger company.... Third, we are operating in a decentralized, profit center fashion, which keeps decision making close to the customer. Finally, the nature of our acquisition program assures that once a business becomes part of the RPM family, it will continue to prosper.[51]

"Well, Tom," Deitz told him, "let me tell you something. I don't think I did anything wrong. And if I get the chance, I'm going to do it again."

Sullivan sat in stunned silence for a moment and then said, "You know, you're right. Bob, how would you like to sell your company to RPM?"

Deitz declined the offer, but Sullivan wouldn't give up that easily. Each year at Christmas, Deitz received a box of chocolates, reminding him that

This photo was taken during RPM's 1994 management meeting. Clockwise from left to right facing the camera are Jeff Stork, Bud Steinberg, and Stephan Rondou. Seated, left to right with their backs to the camera, are Jim Chessin and Piet Jansen.

CHAPTER SEVEN

THE FIRST BILLION

1990 – 1994

Get good people, create a good atmosphere to keep them, and let them do their jobs. It's the same with acquisitions.

—Tom Sullivan quoted in
Chemical Week magazine, 1993

THE BOOMING 1980S SEEMED to end with sudden finality. The Persian Gulf War, fought against Iraq in 1991, and the sting of a sudden recession shook American confidence in the new decade. RPM, however, was protected by its diverse mix of products, both consumer and industrial, and by the noncyclical nature of its offerings.

So instead of lamenting the year gone by, RPM announced at the end of fiscal 1990 that it had just completed its forty-third consecutive year of record sales, earnings, and earnings per share. Again *Financial World* recognized Tom Sullivan's leadership, this time with the bronze medal for "CEO of the Year."

RPM's revenue increases were all the more impressive considering that it had divested about $45 million in businesses that year and that the government was reporting about twenty-six hundred workers were losing their jobs every day.

Kop-Coat and More

After the gradually increasing pace of acquisitions through the late 1980s, 1990 was a particularly busy year, even by RPM standards. That year it negotiated the acquisition of five companies, including Kop-Coat; Aztek Airbrush; Pactra, which Testors acquired; the Briner Paint Manufacturing

Company; and Paramount Technical Products.

Of these, Kop-Coat was the largest, although it was less than one year old. The company, which had 280 employees, started as the coatings division of the Koppers Company, a $2 billion chemical and building product corporation in Pittsburgh. In 1989, however, Koppers was the target of a hostile takeover by British homebuilder Beazer Corporation.[1] During this takeover, Koppers Vice President Charles Pauli negotiated to buy the coatings division for $31 million. He put together a partnership of managers and purely financial backers to raise the money.[2]

"Koppers was the subject of a hostile takeover, so when that happened, I put a plan together to buy the division I was running," Pauli said. "I assembled a corporate team, and we purchased the division. In the meantime, my financial partners thought it was so easy. They had visions of doing crazy things like buying Sherwin-Williams and that type of thing. So I scheduled a meeting with RPM, and the more I looked, the more I thought

---

Tom Sullivan shaking hands with former President Ronald Reagan after RPM was named a bronze medal winner for the chemical industry in *Financial World*'s best-managed companies.

we should sell to RPM. Nine months after we bought it, we sold the company to RPM, and I joined RPM."[3]

RPM paid about $54.5 million for Kop-Coat, which itself had annual sales of $55 million. Its product lines included Wolman wood preservatives; Pettit, Woolsey, and Z-Spar marine products; and Ramuc swimming pool products.[4] Because the division had diverse companies and products, it was partially broken up and merged into existing RPM operating companies. A water and sewage business was turned over to Carboline, and the

swimming pool business was given to Republic Powdered Metals. The division's largest business, Kop-Coat, manufactured a market-leading wood treatment product designed to reduce sap stain on freshly milled lumber.

Shortly before the annual meeting in October 1990, the business section of *USA Today* cited RPM as a safe stock to buy during the hard times. The national newspaper had asked Cleveland-based securities analyst Elliott Schlang to name several companies that had successfully weathered the 1982 recession that were likely to avoid problems during

the one in 1990. "Schlang likes the stock of RPM Inc.," the newspaper said, because it "has shown consistent increases in earnings for the past 43 years."[5] Indeed, an investor who purchased one thousand shares of company stock in the first intrastate offering for $8,000 would have holdings worth more than $1.5 million less than twenty years later.[6]

At the time, RPM listed thirty operating companies and almost $572 million in sales, five times its size ten years before. Still, the corporate staff in Medina was only sixteen people. To avoid expanding its corporate staff, RPM reduced the number

of operating units to twenty, consolidating some of the smaller businesses for financial reporting and planning purposes.[7] It also gave operating company presidents the ability to scout for and negotiate acquisitions on their own. Over the next year more acquisitions were handled at the operating company level.[8]

Paramount Technical Products, which made Paraseal and Superstop foundation waterproofings in Spearfish, North Dakota, was the exception. Handled through the corporate office, the deal brought with it annual sales of about $6 million and a management team under company founder and President Bryan M. McGroarty and Vice President Patrick J. McGroarty.[9]

Rust-Oleum

The trend toward small acquisitions continued into the first half of 1991 as RPM negotiated to buy Zehrung Corporation for $525,000 and Chemical Coatings for $5.023 million. But this pattern wouldn't last long: Tom Sullivan was working on opening a back door to one of RPM's largest acquisitions. Rust-Oleum Corporation, the nation's leading manufacturer of rust-inhibiting paints, was looking to sell its European operation. The company had opened a plant in 1960 in the Netherlands. From there, the European portion of Rust-Oleum, unlike its U.S. counterpart, sold primarily to industrial customers and was virtually unknown to consumers.[10] Rust-Oleum was a privately run company based outside Chicago and owned by the Fergusson family.

At the time, Rust-Oleum wanted to sell only the manufacturing facilities in the Netherlands, its overseas distribution business, and use of the Rust-Oleum name for five years. Sullivan didn't see much value in that package because Europe, and North America as well, already had excess manufacturing capacity and only five years' use of the name wasn't enough. Sullivan countered by asking for a fifty-year licensing agreement and access for

A 1993 photo of Rust-Oleum's packing plant in Roosendaal, the Netherlands. RPM purchased Rust-Oleum's European operation first, hoping for a chance to buy the whole company.

sale in Europe to any new technologies and products Rust-Oleum might develop. For that, he was willing to pay top dollar and offered $34 million in a firm preemptive bid.[11]

The deal was negotiated almost exclusively with Donald Fergusson, grandson of the founder and president, instead of Leonard Judy, then chairman of the board and CEO of the company. In fact, he was on vacation throughout most of the negotiations. When he returned and found out what was happening, Judy hastily arranged a meeting with Fergusson, announcing he didn't like parts of the deal and wanted to reopen negotiations. Sullivan balked.

"Len, you let me walk out of here, and I'm not coming back," Sullivan replied. "You can explain to the Fergusson family why you missed the amount of money we're going to give you."

Sullivan and Jim Karman left to start back to their hotel. Before the day was out, Fergusson again said he needed more money. Sullivan, however, remained firm at $34 million.

"So we argued, and at the end, I'm getting on my coat, and Don Fergusson said, 'OK. 35. I can't go below that.' I said, '34. That's it.' And we're putting on our overcoats. It's winter. He said, 'I can't believe you're walking out of here just on a $1 million difference.' I said, 'No, no, Don, you got that wrong.... I can't believe you're watching me walk out with $34 million in my pocket.'"

But Fergusson let them go—as far as their waiting limousine. While they were getting in, Rust-Oleum's advisor from Merrill Lynch came out and said they had a deal at $34 million.

The Rust-Oleum Effect

Even after the tough negotiation, $34 million was the highest RPM had ever paid, as a multiple of earnings, for any company. But Sullivan was able to justify it because he had his eye on a larger prize: he wanted Rust-Oleum itself and expected the company to go up for sale fairly soon.[12] With Rust-Oleum Europe's $20 million in revenue added to the company's existing international joint ventures, RPM now had a growing presence in Europe.[13]

That year, RPM also sold 50 percent of Euclid Chemical to Swiss Holderbank Financiere Glaris Ltd.[14] This strategic sale was designed to bolster Euclid's international business in concrete additives, which Euclid President Jeffrey Korach expected to grow rapidly.[15]

The Planning Process

The annual planning process that was headed by Jay Morris and Dick Klar was extremely important and one of the prime reasons for RPM's

Rust-Oleum, with its line of rust-preventive and protective consumer paints, was one of the most well-known brands in its industry.

continued success. Executives from each operation would come in for a day to lay out plans on how they were going to grow and protect their margins in the given year.

It was during this process that Jeff Korach explained to Morris and Klar that the major cement companies were not only consolidating vertically by acquiring the ready-mix companies, but were also buying admixture companies, and this could someday greatly affect Euclid Chemical's markets and growth. It was decided that by hooking up with a major cement company, it would not only protect Euclid's market but assist greatly in its growth internationally.

Holderbank was the largest cement company in the world, and in his travels over the previous few years, Sullivan had met its president, Max Amstutz. After the decision to go with a major cement company was made, Karman and Sullivan had dinner with Amstutz in Zurich, Switzerland, two weeks later. A few months after that, RPM sold 50 percent of the Euclid Chemical Company to Holderbank Financiere Glaris Ltd.

All told, 1991 represented another record year. With sales of $500.26 million and earnings of $31.85 million, or $1.03 per share, RPM posted its forty-fourth consecutive record-breaking year. The company had twenty-seven hundred employees at forty-four plants in the United States, Canada, and Europe. International sales were about 10 percent of the total.[16]

Just after announcing these results, in late 1991, RPM moved on another of the industry's most recognized brands. This time, the target was Day-Glo Color Corporation, which RPM bought from Nalco Chemical Company and consolidated with Kop-Coat. Day-Glo had annual sales of about $60 million and a 40 percent market share in fluorescent colorants and pigments.[17] Its headquarters plant was in Cleveland, with a second factory in nearby Twinsburg.[18]

Including Rust-Oleum's European business and Day-Glo, RPM and its subsidiaries made nine acquisitions during 1990 and 1991.[19]

At the company's annual management meeting in the fall of 1991, Sullivan outlined the plans to take RPM to its first billion dollars in sales over the next five years, ending with a prediction of sales reaching $2 billion by 2001. The five-year fore-casts of the company's growth, which began in 1971, had proven to be extremely accurate.

Frank's First Deal

Continuing to bolster its international presence, RPM pursued more international companies in 1992. The largest was Martin Mathys N.V. of Halen, Belgium, which made and distributed protective coatings for buildings in Belgium, France, Germany, and the Netherlands. The company had begun in 1845 and had annual sales of $24 million. Because it was located in Belgium, there were special circumstances surrounding the acquisition, recalled Joe Ciulla, a long-time outside accountant for RPM.

"We bought Martin Mathys for $36 million, which included $18 million in cash," he said. "In Belgium, if you own stock in a company and you sell the stock, there are no capital gains if you sell it to another Belgian corporation. If you sell it to other than a Belgian corporation, you would end up paying a tremendous amount of tax. So we structured it so there wouldn't be any tax for them."[20]

The deal was also significant for another reason: It marked Frank Sullivan's first major business deal. The young Frank had joined RPM in 1987 through its roofing joint venture in North Carolina and had quickly risen to vice president of corporate development.

Soon after the Martin Mathys acquisition, Bud Steinberg, in the Carboline subsidiary, negotiated the acquisition of Century Polymers, a Freeport, Texas, company that made coatings for flooring and lining applications. Cofounder and President Ray Stavinoha joined RPM.[21] This move was followed in December 1992 by the acquisition of Mantrose-Haeuser for $9.525 million.

"One of the Best Managed"

In 1992, RPM paid an honor to its loyal investors when it elected Lorrie Gustin, a director of the National Association of Investment Clubs (NAIC), to the board of directors. At the time, RPM stock ranked fourth in the holdings of NAIC club members, and the company had maintained a friendly relationship with the organization.[22] Gustin had, in fact, urged Karman to attend his first NAIC meeting in 1974, thus beginning RPM's mutually benefi-cial relationship with small investors. "I've been to every convention," Karman said in 2000, "and I'm probably the only president or CEO who's been there for twenty-six years in a row."[23]

At the annual meeting, the board of directors voted a 50 percent stock dividend and raised its quarterly cash dividend to 18 cents a share, mark-ing nineteen consecutive years of dividend increases and the ninth major stock dividend.[24]

In a profile in *Chemical Week* magazine in early 1993, an analyst called the company "one of the best-managed companies in the country." In the article, Tom Sullivan likened the company's acquisition strategy to the "people" strategy of his father: "Get good people, create a good atmosphere to keep them, and let them do their jobs. It's the same with acquisitions," he said, citing the drive to acquire well-managed companies with managers eager to join the RPM family.[25]

"I think of RPM as almost a mutual fund of businesses," said analyst Jerry H. Dombcik of McDonald & Company of Cleveland. Dombcik also praised RPM's intuition about when to get out of a business. He noted that RPM had stripped away businesses with $100 million in sales as the busi-nesses lost profitability.[26]

A few months later, Jim Karman, using RPM as his model, told a group of investors and entre-preneurs how to shape a company that will be attractive to investors. "Have a product that is not price sensitive, has good quality, and can be explained easily," he said.[27]

Moving on Bondo and Stonhard

If RPM could be characterized as a mutual fund, it was an exceptionally focused one. In 1993, Sullivan and Karman continued to expand in the specialty coating industry with two major acquisitions: the Dynatron/Bondo Corporation, and Stonhard.

Dynatron/Bondo was best known for Bondo, a polyester-based compound that was the leading auto body repair filler. The firm sold similar prod-ucts to body shops under the Dynatron name. Based in Atlanta and run by founder and President Quin Machamer, the company had annual sales of $45 mil-lion. RPM paid $43.2 million for it.[28] Dynatron/Bondo fit strategically with Talsol, which made Mar-Hyde

automotive paints, and RPM's marine product lines, including Pettit, Woolsey, and Z-Spar.[29]

Stonhard, based in Maple Shade, New Jersey, was RPM's entrée into the industrial flooring market. Founded in 1922, Stonhard was a leading manufac-turer of industrial and commercial polymer flooring. It boasted sales of $100 million a year, and RPM paid $105 million in stock to purchase the company. Its product line included the high-end Stonlux line of antistatic flooring used by the electronics industry. At the time of the acquisition, the company was run by Jeffrey M. Stork, president and son of the founder; Don Zickman, in charge of sales; and Dave Reif, CFO.

"Several companies were interested in buying us, but RPM was our clear choice for two main rea-sons," recalled Stork. "I liked the autonomy RPM gives its operating companies and the performance of RPM's stock. Essentially, I traded stock in a privately held company for RPM stock that has had consistent growth."[30]

Reif, who later transferred to RPM corporate as CFO, then back to Stonhard as president, remem-bered the case that Tom and Frank Sullivan pre-sented during the negotiations. "It was a good choice for us because Tom and Frank said we could sell the company, liquidate, get the cash out of it, but then stay with the company and run it," Reif said. "Our job was to grow the company, and they would take over balance-sheet responsibilities."[31]

Year-End

The rapid growth of the previous few years and Frank Sullivan's growing importance to the company were reflected in the expansion of RPM's corporate staff. Charles P. Brush was named vice president of environmental affairs; Glenn R. Hasman was promoted from controller to vice pres-ident of administration; Keith R. Smiley took over as controller; and Frank Sullivan was promoted from vice president of corporate development to chief financial officer.[32]

RPM's 1993 sales of $625.7 million earned it the 491st spot on the prestigious *Fortune* 500 list of the U.S.'s largest industrial companies. RPM's $39.4 million in profits placed it at number 265.[33] Once all the new acquisitions were figured in, the restated revenue leapt to $768.4 million with earnings of $39.5 million, an astonishing 33 percent single-year gain.[34]

The Rest of Rust-Oleum

In January 1994, Sullivan's foresight paid off when the $140 million Rust-Oleum Corporation declared it was for sale. The Fergusson family, which owned the company for three generations, hired Lehman Brothers' investment banking

---

It wasn't uncommon for RPM to begin shopping for a company decades before a purchase could be arranged. Such was the case with Tremco, whose founder had worked with Frank J. Sullivan at Arco Paint Company at the turn of the century. RPM would finally realize its chance in the late 1990s.

services to find a buyer. Initially, Rust-Oleum had considered holding a public offering or selling part of the company to employees but finally decided to find a larger partner in the rapidly consolidating paint business.[35]

By this time, Sullivan had been courting the Fergusson family for fifteen years and hoped he could arrange a privately negotiated deal before Rust-Oleum was put on the auction block. "I had been through four chairmen at Rust-Oleum," Sullivan said. Unfortunately, however, there was no preemptive deal.[36]

Later, Sullivan would look back on the negotiations to buy Rust-Oleum as one of the strangest in his business life. It was also the first time RPM hired an investment banking advisor. The advisor was John Herrmann, who had recently worked for Lehman Brothers and been involved earlier with

RPM in the 1985 Carboline acquisition. When he heard RPM was interested in Rust-Oleum, Herrmann called Sullivan with an offer to represent the company during negotiations.

"John, you know how we price things," Sullivan answered. "You know who's involved with it. Strictly me. You know that we don't need brokers."[37]

But Herrmann thought he could be of help because he had intimate knowledge of the people at Lehman. Sullivan still wasn't interested. Then Herrmann made Sullivan an offer he couldn't refuse: "Let me represent you in my way, and then at the end, if you get it, you give me what you think I'm worth. If it's worth nothing, give me nothing."[38]

So in late March 1994, Sullivan led an RPM team that included John Herrmann into a meeting with Rust-Oleum's negotiating team. There the RPM team was surprised to meet Anthony "The Pelican" Pellicano Jr., a childhood friend of Don Fergusson. Pellicano had no financial background, but he was an intimidating figure nonetheless. He worked in Hollywood, and his specialty was said to be digging up incriminating or embarrassing information on people.[39] Pellicano reportedly bragged to a newspaper that although he didn't carry a gun, he could put a pencil through a person's heart in two seconds.

"So that was rule number one," Sullivan remembered. "Don't carry pencils into the negotiation."[40] Things got off to a rough start anyway when Pellicano, just after being introduced to Sullivan, asked "How's your mother in the hospital doing?"

Sullivan was taken aback. "My mother had just been hospitalized," he said. "He was letting me know he knew something about me and my personal life. It only hardened the negotiations."[41]

Soon after the discussion began, it became clear that Pellicano was calling the shots, and that he was expecting to get somewhere above $200 million for Rust-Oleum. But Sullivan felt that was too high. During due diligence, RPM's lawyers and accountants had uncovered accounting errors that negatively affected the earnings picture Rust-Oleum was presenting. Because of the discrepancy, Sullivan said the highest he would offer was $190 million.

Pellicano wasn't interested, so the RPM team walked out of negotiations and headed for a private party at Harry Caray's, a landmark Chicago restaurant.[42] Soon after, Sullivan and his team flew back to Cleveland, and then Sullivan went on to Florida. "It haunted me for about a week," he recalled, "then I finally got rid of it. I had just walked away from what was the biggest acquisition in my life. I thought, 'You're probably dumb.'"[43]

But the story wasn't over yet. In late April, Frank Sullivan poked his head into his dad's office and said, "Dad, I probably have done something wrong. You're probably going to get mad at me."

Frank, after hearing nothing further about the sale of Rust-Oleum, even when the deadline for bids had passed, had called John Herrmann and asked him to find out what was going on. Herrmann soon told Frank that no deal was in the works, not for $190 million and certainly not for $200 million, so an RPM bid of $190 million could likely take Rust-Oleum.[44]

Tom Sullivan was interested and told Frank to see if a deal for $180 million could fly.[45]

Before long, Tom Sullivan was heading back to Chicago, where Herrmann told him that Pellicano would once again be part of the negotiations. "You know what I'm going to do?" Sullivan asked Herrmann rhetorically. "I'm going to get this below 180 because they're in a corner, and the Pelican put them there." Seeing Sullivan's mood, Herrmann suggested that Sullivan stay away from the negotiations. "This can't come down to a matter of pride," Herrmann said. "It's got to come down to a matter of dollars and cents, and if you're not there staring at the Pelican, and he's not there staring at you, we'll take pride off the table."

"Great," Sullivan replied. "I want it down to 175."

"You're making this difficult," Herrmann said.

"I don't give a damn," Sullivan said, but he agreed to stay out of the room.

Two hours later, the phone rang in Sullivan's hotel room. "I got this to 177," Herrmann told him.

Sullivan responded: "176."

"You're being a jerk here," said Herrmann.

"176.5."

"Why don't you give a little bit?" Herrmann asked.

"No."

"I'll call you right back."[46]

The deal finally closed at $176.5 million, giving RPM one of the most recognizable brands in the consumer paint business. The Rust-Oleum acquisition represented a sea change in RPM's

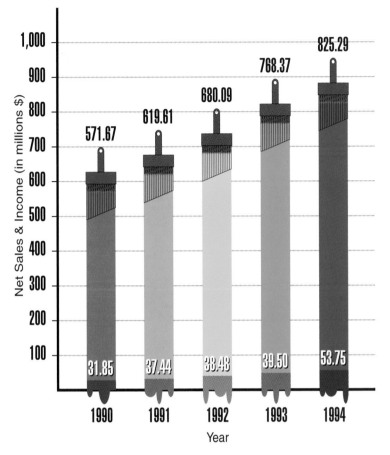

sumer outlets. After the deal closed, Tom Sullivan asked Mike Tellor, then Carboline's executive vice president, to move to Chicago as president of Rust-Oleum.

"Rust-Oleum was not the most customer-intimate company," Tellor remembered.

After the acquisition, we did some studies with customers and found out what they liked about us and what they didn't like about us, and the company's inflexibility came out loud and strong. We were a rust-preventative company and that was it. We decided that if we were going to grow, we've got to be more than just rust preventative. We had to get into other sections of our category, which we defined as small project painting. So, besides being rust preventative, there's a decorative section, a professional section, and a general purpose section, and that's where we need to have our products.[47]

With Dynatron/Bondo, Stonhard, and Rust-Oleum, RPM was at the top of its game. In 1994, the company posted sales of $815.6 million and $52.6 million in net income. Better yet, many of RPM's products, whether industrial or consumer, held a commanding market lead.

profile because it was by far the largest consumer company RPM had ever pursued. It would require a fundamental change in the way RPM approached distribution to hardware stores and other con-

Tom Sullivan and Jim Karman at RPM's 50th anniversary management meeting.

CHAPTER EIGHT

THE RIGHT MARKETS

1995–1997

For hitting fifty years of record sales and record earnings, we ought to celebrate.

—Tom Sullivan, 1997

RPM BEGAN 1995 WITH ONE of industrial America's most admired financial records. With sales expected to top $1 billion that year, the company enjoyed praise from almost every quarter. In January, RPM joined the NASDAQ 100 Index, which measured the performance of nonfinancial stocks traded in NASDAQ stock.[1]

In March, the Harvard Business School Club of Cleveland recognized Tom Sullivan's achievement with the 1995 Business Statesman Award. The honor recognized a chief executive for a combination of business success and community activity.[2] A few months later, the company again was named a "Dividend Achiever" by Moody's Investors Service. Moody's designation went to only 331 of the 10,000 public companies. To qualify, a company had to increase dividends for ten straight years.[3]

Enjoying one of the best U.S. economies in decades, RPM saw nothing on the horizon that would threaten this record. The paint industry was growing steadily though not rapidly, with the market for specialty coatings somewhat exceeding the general growth rate. Impact Marketing Consultants, a research firm, said paint industry revenue would grow at an average rate of 2.1 percent annually from 1996 to 2001. Specialty paints, by contrast, were predicted to grow at a 3.8 percent rate.[4]

Dryvit Systems

As always, one of the keys to RPM's sustained growth was acquisitions, leading the company in 1995 to issue $150 million in ten-year, 7 percent bonds. The money was designed not to buy new companies but to restructure RPM's existing debt at a lower interest rate, thereby giving RPM additional borrowing power to buy more companies.

One of the intended targets was Dryvit Systems, which RPM purchased in 1995 for $105 million. Dryvit was a leading maker of exterior insulation and finishing systems (EIFS) used in commercial and residential construction. The company had annual sales of about $70 million. Paul H. Hill agreed to stay with Dryvit as president.[5]

Dryvit was one of those deals that almost didn't happen. Early that summer, Sullivan had begun negotiations in a preemptive bid for the company. When another bid materialized, however, RPM withdrew from the discussions. A few weeks later, with Sullivan and his son Frank deeply involved in the bond issue, Hill called Frank Sullivan.

This image, stressing the global reach of RPM's brands, appeared on the cover of the 1996 annual report.

Dryvit's exterior coatings were used extensively throughout the plush New York–New York megahotel and casino in Las Vegas, Nevada, as well as virtually every new casino complex built there in the past decade.

"Frank, guess what?" he said. "The auction is not going as hoped and management prefers RPM—if you want Dryvit, it's available."[6] Tom Sullivan was ready to jump, but he had a problem. Chase Manhattan Bank would sell the bond notes only with the understanding that the money from the notes would be used to retire debt and for other internal purposes but *not* for acquisitions. Not only would using the money increase RPM's debt to unacceptable levels, but it would look as if Tom and Frank Sullivan had gone back on their word.

"We went back to the Dryvit people and said, 'We can do this only if you take half in stock and half in cash,'" Tom Sullivan said. "They did it. So we maintained our debt ratio, and we maintained our story. We got hold of Dryvit and didn't lose our credibility. In fact, we gained some because we showed people we were willing to work within boundaries."[7]

Breaking the Billion Dollar Barrier

In July 1995, RPM proved the analysts right when it announced that sales for the year would surpass $1 billion. At $1.016 billion, 1995's sales were 25 percent higher than the previous year's results, partially because of continued success with Rust-Oleum, which boasted more than $200 million annually in revenue, and partially because of the torrid pace of acquisitions throughout the year. In 1995 alone, RPM purchased six companies, including Dryvit, for a total of almost $140 million. The new companies included Espan, PTE Ltd.; Simian Company; the WOODLIFE product line; Star Finishing Products; and the PLASTIC WOOD product line.

Although breaking the billion-dollar barrier was a significant milestone, the achievement didn't make the cover of the 1995 annual report. Instead, the company used the space to reiterate the philosophy that Frank C. Sullivan built his company on: "Hire the best people you can find. Create an atmosphere that will keep them. Then let them do their jobs."[8]

These words had perhaps never been more well timed. Poised at the billion dollar mark, RPM was standing at the brink of major changes, both internal and external. One of these changes would be leadership: In October 1995, Frank C. Sullivan, the founder's namesake and Tom Sullivan's son, was named executive vice president and elected to the company's board of directors.[9]

Another adjustment was RPM's changing profile. For a long time, RPM had sought out family-run, small, entrepreneurial companies as targets for acquisition. As RPM had grown, however, so had the size of its target companies. Instead of being run by founders and entrepreneurs, these companies were often run by professional managers. Already RPM's corporate office had begun to grow and evolve.

RPM was beginning to experience the challenges and potential inefficiencies that come with size. The consolidation really began overseas, which was perhaps logical since RPM risked the least in these markets. In 1990, total overseas sales stood at $25.6 million, representing only 5.6 percent of total sales. By 1995, these figures had grown to $117.6 million, or 11.6 percent of total sales, and were continuing to rise.[10]

That year, the company bought its Singapore distributor, Espan, managed by Javis Lim. Tom Sullivan Jr., along

with his wife Mary, moved to Singapore to oversee the rapid expansion for RPM in Southeast Asia. After a three-year stint, with sales tripling in the area, Tom and Mary moved back to Cleveland, Ohio, where he became director of development for the Tremco Group of companies.

To achieve the best results from these far-flung businesses, RPM established the "Do-It-Yourself Council," which pulled in representatives from operating companies to plan a variety of overseas marketing initiatives for consumer products, including shared trade show booths and joint sales calls. These efforts were quick to bear fruit: in 1996, overseas sales reached $200 million, or 18 percent of total sales.

Back in the United States, it would be much harder for RPM's traditionally separate operating companies to collaborate. But collaboration was becoming increasingly necessary. By the mid-1990s, the company was seeking ways to use the collective strength of its many operating companies. "We have accelerated efforts to capitalize on

---

This letter was included as part of Michael Jordan's book on success, which Tom Sullivan presented to RPM employees as a gift and motivational tool.

RPM

RPM, INC. · 2628 Pearl Road · P.O. Box 777 · Medina, Ohio 44258 · 216·273·8800

Thomas C. Sullivan
Chairman

Dear RPM Associate:

I've told the story on many occasions how on the evening after my father's burial, August 18, 1971, while sitting on Jim Karman's porch, I commented that RPM would have to grow from its sales of $11 million to $50 million in five years or the company would be sold.

By 1976 that goal had been met. We then reasoned that if RPM grew by 15 percent a year, we would double our size every five years.

In just under 20 years, RPM has attained two goals which, undoubtedly, would have been thought of as too "lofty" back in 1976. In April of 1994, RPM was included for the first time in the *Fortune 500*; and for fiscal year ending May 31, 1995, sales will reach one billion dollars.

This has been achieved because we focused on the near-term goals and, at the same time, remained faithful to the philosophy laid down by my father —go out and get good people, create the atmosphere to keep good people, and let them do their work.

I am truly grateful for your help in making this happen.

Sincerely yours,

RPM, INC.

Thomas C. Sullivan

TCS/mkh

the intellectual assets within groups of RPM businesses that address common markets and share common technologies," Tom Sullivan wrote in the 1996 annual report.[11]

To this end, RPM took its first steps toward uniting parts of its domestic companies. The RPM Technical Council was founded to share "ideas, problems, and opportunities" among the research and development directors at operating companies. Similarly, the RPM Purchasing Action Council looked to use leveraged buying power to save money on individual operating companies' material costs, and the RPM International Managers Conference brought together all the international sales managers for an annual meeting.

The next step was to group RPM's operating companies into reporting groups, combining businesses with similar customer groups and channels of distribution. This reduced the number of units reporting directly to headquarters.[12]

TCI and Okura

Consolidation, however, was more of a quest for efficiency. Growth would come through continued strategic acquisitions. In 1996, RPM made four acquisitions, the largest of which were TCI in January and Okura Holdings in June.

TCI, based in Ellaville, Georgia, was bought in a stock swap valued at about $35 million. TCI's line of powdered coatings designed primarily for automakers represented a new product area. In the past, Sullivan had told reporters that he was considering moving into the fast-growing powdered automotive coatings business but was leery because the automotive business was so cyclical.

"We don't like original equipment manufacturing," Sullivan said at the 1995 annual meeting.[13] But TCI proved to be the exception. During the acquisition, its management team, led by Thomas H. Slade, remained in place. Revenue for 1996 was estimated to hit about $20 million.[14]

Larger still was the purchase of Okura, a manufacturer of fiberglass-reinforced grating products (used for pedestrian walkways, staircases, and other applications) sold under the Fibergrate

and Chemgrate brand names.[15] Based in Dallas, Okura had sales of $35 million in 1995. The company had three domestic manufacturing plants, plus operations in Shanghai, China, and Terneuzen, Holland. An investment group, Cortec Group Fund, had owned Okura.[16]

RPM saw an opportunity to sell the Fibergrate and Chemgrate products to the same customers that were targeted by Stonhard, which was planning to introduce a new epoxy terrazzo floor, and Carboline into the oil and chemical markets.[17]

The two smaller acquisitions were those of Dryvit Poland, an overseas unit of Dryvit, and Chemrite Coatings, a South African licensee that sold Carboline products throughout South Africa.

Tremco

The year 1996 again produced record results, but earnings growth—still a respectable 6 percent—was not enough to satisfy RPM management or the key analysts following the company. There were a variety of reasons for the decline in the growth of earnings, including an unusually severe winter that curtailed the home maintenance season.[18] Still, investors questioned Tom Sullivan and Jim Karman closely in early 1997 during a conference sponsored by Merrill Lynch & Company. One analyst, noting that all RPM companies were put on "Plan B" in 1996 because of the disappointing growth in earnings, asked Sullivan about the company's efforts to control its costs and incentivize its company heads.

Sullivan responded by talking about cost-cutting structures, including some of the more recent attempts at consolidation, and the strong growth in overseas markets. He noted that RPM had recently changed its compensation and incentive program for operating presidents, urging them toward 10 percent annual growth.[19]

Tom Sullivan's foresight paid off in 1994, when RPM was able to acquire all of Rust-Oleum, thus gaining a major foothold in the paint sections of home improvement stores.

More importantly, Sullivan was able to show off RPM's latest prize: Tremco. RPM announced the October 1996 letter of intent to buy Tremco from BFGoodrich, which was shedding businesses outside the chemical and aerospace sectors.[20]

With a price tag of $236 million, Tremco was RPM's largest acquisition to date and, according to accountant Joe Ciulla and Executive Vice President Jay Morris, "probably the greatest acquisition RPM ever made."[21] The company made sealants and coatings for the construction and maintenance industries and boasted annual sales of $350 million. Like many other companies, Tremco had been on Tom Sullivan's shopping list for several decades. His father, Frank Sullivan, had even worked with Tremco's founder, William Treuhaft, at Atlantic Refining in the 1910s. In 1979, Tremco was sold to BFGoodrich to avoid a hostile takeover.[22]

The deal that united RPM and Tremco began on a Friday afternoon in late 1996 when John Ong, Goodrich's chairman, called Tom Sullivan to solicit an offer. "Why don't you look at our information," Ong told Sullivan, "and based on this, I want you to come back and tell me what you think you're willing to pay, and if that works, we will then sit down and negotiate a deal."[23]

Interested in the deal, Tom Sullivan, Jim Karman, Frank Sullivan, and Bill Papenbrock next met with Ong and Goodrich President David L. Burner. "For whatever reason, still not fully known to me, [Ong and Burner] wanted to do a lot of this without getting their people involved," Tom Sullivan remembered. "They were acting like the entrepreneurs we're used to dealing with. And they wanted us to do a purchase agreement without completely doing due diligence. We've never done that before, and common sense would tell you that's really not the thing to do."[24]

The RPM team put together a purchase agreement but insisted on a side letter that allowed them to renegotiate the price should due diligence turn up anything that substantially affected the value of the Tremco properties. After rigorous negotiations and many hard-fought battles over a number of points and issues, the deal closed, and RPM had completed an unusual trifecta.[25]

At one time, Tremco, Carboline, and RPM had been the three largest players in the industrial coatings market. As of 1997, both former RPM

Tremco sealants were used throughout the Petronas Office Towers in Kuala Lumpur City Centre in Malaysia. The towers are the world's tallest buildings.

competitors wrote home to Medina, and the acquisition was widely praised both inside and outside RPM. "Tremco is a wonderful company with great sales," Karman said.[26]

Similarly, Karen Gilsenan, a Merrill Lynch analyst, liked the move. "Tremco will have higher earnings under RPM than it did with Goodrich," she told Chemical Week magazine. "In the short term, the acquisition is a big one and levels up RPM's balance sheet. RPM will shed businesses that are not up to par to clean up its balance sheet."[27]

Reorganizing the Business

In fact, by the end of 1997, RPM's debt load had again increased significantly, causing Moody's Investors Service to inquire about the company's

The snow-covered RPM headquarters building in 1995. By this time, the staff in the corporate office had grown beyond the fifteen or sixteen long-time employees but was still extremely small given RPM's size and complexity.

president and president of the Tremco Sealants Group.[31] Dick Klar, an RPM vice president who was managing the planning process with Morris, became Tremco's CFO.[32]

Finally, RPM reorganized its own structure to accommodate Tremco. Republic Powdered Metals, the original roofing materials business, combined with Mameco and Tremco to create the Tremco Group.[33] This gave RPM one of the country's broadest lines of roofing products, including hot and cold built-up roofs, modified bitumen roofing, single-ply roofing membranes, and sealants and adhesives.[34]

While the Tremco acquisition and the merging of various businesses brought great opportunities,

Left: The World Trade Center in Beijing, pictured in 1997. Tremco sealant products were used during construction of the building. With the Tremco acquisition complete, RPM had purchased one of its largest competitors.

Below: The Hawaii Convention Center in Honolulu, Hawaii. The innovative building uses both Carboline corrosion control coatings and Dryvit exterior insulation finishing systems.

credit rating. Even without Tremco, RPM had a busy year, racking up nine mostly international acquisitions for more than $32 million.[28] But the increased debt load was only temporary. RPM moved quickly to revitalize Tremco, by far the largest drain on its balance sheet, and maximize the company's contribution to RPM.

First, RPM sold off a group of Tremco's businesses totaling about $111 million—making the net cost of the acquisition only $125 million—and cut sixty administrative positions at Tremco's headquarters. The divested companies included Swiggle Insulating Glass, sold to a Cleveland investment firm,[29] and Tremco's Auto Replacement Glass, sold for about $4 million.[30]

Next, in an unusual departure from RPM's traditional approach, Tremco's management was reorganized. Jeffrey L. Korach, president of Euclid Chemical, was named president of Tremco. James L. Chessin, president of Mameco, became Tremco vice

Above: The Al Hana Mosque, in Malaysia, is protected by Mameco sealants.

Right: At a trade show in Asia, buyers visit the Euclid Chemical booth.

it also had its challenges. As Frank Sullivan put it, "I will never forget standing in the big picture window on the second floor landing of the corporate office and watching Tom personally walk up to the Republic Powdered Metals building to deliver the news to the Republic management team that they would be downsized and integrated and moved to the Tremco headquarters. His willingness to make this change with the founding company and his insistence on personally and candidly communicating this difficult decision has been a hallmark of his success."[35]

At the same time, RPM sold other underperforming companies and negotiated several smaller acquisitions. Divestitures included Craft House,[36] which produced the Paint-by-Numbers kits and other hobby products, and two resin plants operated by Rust-Oleum[37] and Zinsser, respectively.

These companies, particularly the resin plants, were outside RPM's core competency.[38]

These moves had the effect of changing RPM's product mix. At the end of 1997, about 60 percent of RPM's business was maintenance and protection coatings for industrial customers. The other 40 percent was consumer-oriented products. The company's products were sold in 130 countries and manufactured in fifty-nine plants.[39]

RPM's ongoing effort to "maximize its intellectual capital" at the individual operating companies continued. In 1997, Tom Sullivan said in the company's annual report that "while it's difficult to quantify the cumulative effect of inter-company cooperation, specific instances suggest an operating profit impact of several million dollars."[40]

The Fiftieth Anniversary

Traditionally, the company showed its appreciation to the one thousand or so shareholders who attended the annual meetings by giving them a bucket filled with RPM's latest products. These gifts were popular, but for RPM's fiftieth anniver-

To celebrate its fiftieth anniversary, RPM hired the Cleveland Orchestra to play at the shareholders' meeting. After an unexpected number of shareholders requested tickets, the concert performance was moved from Severance Hall to the Cleveland State Convocation Center. During the party, Tom Sullivan's family was recognized. Pictured, inset, standing from left are Jack and Sue Jacobus, Dave and Kaki O'Neill, Father Sean Sullivan, and Jim and Joan Livingston. Patty O'Neill is seated at right. Seated at left are members of Jim Karman's family, including from left Craig Cook, Jan Karman Cook, and Carol Karman.

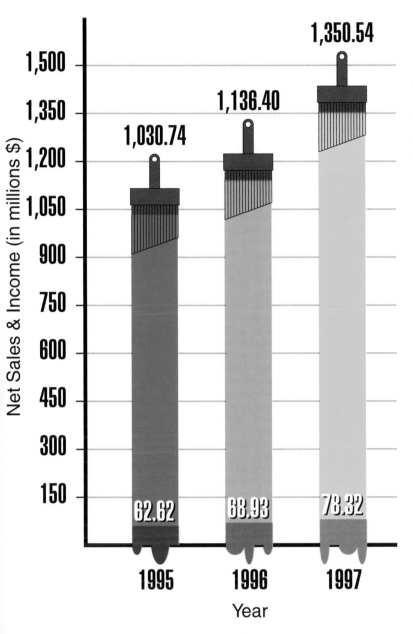

Net Sales & Income (in millions $)

1,350.54

1,136.40

1,030.74

62.62   68.93   78.32

1,500

1,350

1,200

1,050

900

750

600

450

300

150

1995   1996   1997

Year

RPM's sales and earnings for 1995 through 1997. Earnings are represented by the darker area within the sales bar.

During a special ceremony in New York City, RPM was recognized for this achievement by Frank Zarb, chairman of the National Association of Securities Dealers. To Sullivan, it seemed only fitting that RPM throw a great big party for itself.

"I've had a couple of shareholders write and say we're trying to massage our already big egos," Sullivan said at the time. "My answer is that for hitting fifty years of record sales and record earnings, we ought to celebrate."[41] To do this, RPM enlisted the help of the renowned Cleveland Orchestra. Kathie M. Rogers, manager of investor relations and Jim Karman's longtime assistant, helped plan the day.

"The event was supposed to be at Severance Hall, which is the home of the Cleveland Orchestra," Rogers said. "So we sent out a notice that the annual meeting would be at Severance Hall because the Cleveland Orchestra will play, but for this event, you would need a ticket. Well, the requests started coming in, and I was like, 'Gosh.' I went in to Tom and said, 'We've got kind of a problem. We've got about four thousand requests for tickets for the annual meeting, but Severance Hall only holds twenty-three hundred.'"

To remedy the situation, RPM wanted to move the event to the Cleveland State Convocation Center, a new venue with good acoustics. After testing the sound, the orchestra agreed—a rarity in itself—and RPM hosted its annual meeting for about five thousand pleased shareholders.

"It was fabulous," Rogers remembered. "We even made the *New York Times* because it was unheard of to have an orchestra play at an annual meeting."[42]

sary, Tom Sullivan was looking for something a little bigger. The company, after all, was celebrating fifty consecutive years of record sales and earnings—and even Nasdaq was excited about it.

In 1998, RPM, Inc., was listed on the New York Stock Exchange. Pictured are Jim Karman and Tom Sullivan celebrating.

CHAPTER NINE

RPM RISING

1998–2001

*For the thirty years Tom Sullivan was at the helm, he's created suc-
cess in a manner that has a whole lot more to do with trusting people
and believing in them than with financial focus.*

—Frank Sullivan, 2001

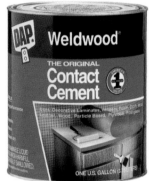

HEADING INTO 1998, RPM'S
record string of increased revenue and earnings would continue, but not without growing pains.
By the mid- and late-1990s, RPM's
markets and distribution were changing rapidly, especially where some of
its most recognizable brands were con-
cerned. As in its own industry, consolidation was
sweeping through the consumer home improvement
business. But instead of a large corporation buying the small outlets, the smaller stores were being
replaced by cavernous home improvement centers
such as Home Depot, Lowes, and others.

More and more of RPM's product lines were
being concentrated under the roofs of these popular
new stores, which was both good and bad for RPM.
Rust-Oleum, for instance, enjoyed a whopping 17
percent sales increase in 1997, the year that it became
a category manager for Home Depot. This market
alone was worth about $70 million in sales.

However, due to Home Depot's structured relationship with its suppliers, profit margins were
lower than RPM's shareholders were used to. Home
Depot had pioneered supplier seminars in which
companies competed for space on Home Depot's
shelves in cutthroat single-day sales presentations,
with Home Depot buying agents aggressively negotiating for the best price.

RPM was not at Home Depot's mercy, however.
With brands like Rust-Oleum and Day-Glo, RPM

had tremendous name recognition with
consumers. "Paint is a big draw," Jim
Karman said. "People go in those stores
for paint, and we have five different ways
to reach a consumer. We can organize
that department for them. So we have
some leverage."[1]

Home Depot also required that its
vendors ship straight to the stores, meaning that it
was logical for RPM to reconsider its small-factory
shipments in favor of centralized distribution for its
big customers. "We have had to expand our facilities to accommodate Home Depot's direct-to-store
mentality," said Bob Senior, president of Zinsser.
Home Depot remained Zinsser's largest customer.[2]

The Benefits of Bigness

But what was true for the giant retailers was
also true for RPM: size had its own advantages.
By 1998, RPM had sixty-eight hundred employees and sold products in more than 130 countries. That year, the company switched from the
Nasdaq to the New York Stock Exchange under
the symbol RPM.

In 1999, RPM announced the purchase of DAP for $290 million.
DAP was a well-known consumer brand of caulks, sealants, and
related products that had major distribution.

At the same time, the company was getting used to the idea of consolidation. So far, the limited attempts at cooperation among the operating companies had proven successful. The Purchasing Action Council, for example, saved $6 million—Testors alone saved $500,000—by sharing tooling with another operating company.

So now RPM was ready to take the major organizational step of knitting its operating companies together. With such empowered operating company presidents, the move carried with it an element of risk. But Sullivan and Karman were convinced it was the right thing to do, and they announced

that RPM was being reorganized into two broad operating units: the Industrial Division and the Consumer Division.[3]

"With RPM's sales growing by nearly $1 billion over the past five years and anticipated strong sales growth ahead, we organized RPM into two separate units," Sullivan and Karman told shareholders in 1998. "We now have one group of operating companies that addresses primarily industrial markets, while the other group sells primarily to the consumer retail marketplace."[4]

The Industrial Division included Tremco, Stonhard, Carboline, Dryvit, and Day-Glo. Jay Morris took the reins of this group.

The Consumer Division brought together Bondo/Mar-Hyde, Rust-Oleum, Testors, Zinsser, and the wood-finishing businesses, under the direction of Kenneth M. Evans. The Consumer Division

RPM staff gathered on June 9, 1998, to celebrate the first time RPM rode the Big Board, while Karman, Sullivan, and others attended the formalities in New York (inset). With its superior performance, RPM's stock kept its loyal following among investment clubs.

represented about half of RPM's overall business. Evans, former chairman and CEO of Armor All Products Corporation, was nearing retirement but signed on with RPM to help the company plan its major strategic shift.

"We developed a systemic approach to sourcing, developing, and commercializing new products, to finding ways for the laboratories to connect with sales and marketing so that the right products were on the market, and to developing consumer research and exploiting the product to its fullest extent," Evans said. "RPM had sixty-one plants acquired over many years, and there was probably redundancy there. We also took a look at some of the expense areas that weren't directly impacting the customer."[5]

To handle the centralization, the corporate staff was bolstered and the reporting lines were further streamlined. For the first time, operating company presidents didn't all report to Jay Morris at headquarters, and new executives moved into upper management. Charles G. Pauli, president of the Kop-Coat business group, which included Alox and Day-Glo, was named vice president—technology, retaining his other duties. David Reif

Above: Day-Glo products could be found in thousands of places where color was important. This plane uses fluorescent tracer pigments to help firefighters determine areas already sprayed with fire retardants.

Below: Product innovation continued within the operating companies. Pictured is Testors Aztek airbrush, which was designed to help hobbyists apply model paint.

RETURNING TO NURTURE ONE'S ROOTS

JOSE GONZALEZ'S FIRST DAY AS A FIFTH grader was a nightmare. He didn't want to look at anyone, and he didn't want to speak. He wanted to run, to run away and hide. Jose, who grew up in Cleveland's economically disadvantaged West Side, was painfully shy.

But Jose had another attribute: he was lucky. Lucky because events had brought him to the Urban Community School—the nation's oldest inner-city, multicultural community school. For many of its 408 students, the imaginary monsters of childhood are real. Three out of four of them come from families living at or below the federal poverty level. To get to school the children traverse a veritable wasteland of economic and social collapse: abandoned buildings, graffiti-decorated housing projects, homeless shelters, soup kitchens, and too many people who have no place to live. Urban Community School stands as a safe haven where children of all ethnicities and religious persuasions come to learn.

Founded in 1968 by the Ursuline Sisters of Cleveland, the school, which teaches youngsters from three years of age through the eighth grade, is remarkable in several ways. Although supported by the Ursuline nuns, it honors the faith traditions of all who enter its doors. It does not promote a particular religion; rather, students receive religious instruction according to their family's faith tradition. And the school is devoted to meeting each child at the child's educational level. If a child in seventh grade reads at a fourth-grade level, the teachers begin to teach the child at the fourth grade level and work to move forward from there. Also, the school is nongraded. Sister Maureen Doyle, who runs the school, explained that children are not graded "because so many of our children come from an environment where failure has been part of their life." The Urban Community School is commit-

ted to changing that equation with a special type of education that can address the needs of children like Jose Gonzales.

For Jose, that help came in the person of Sister Mary, his teacher. She immediately took a liking to the shy, skinny boy, and she started to encourage him. She challenged him to mature. "She showed me how to grow up outside the classroom, to grow up socially," Jose said.

With Sister Mary's encouragement, Jose's behavior changed. He tried out for the basketball team and made it. Gradually, the prospect of meeting new people and making new friends didn't seem so bad.

Kids like Jose were surprisingly easy for Tom Sullivan to understand. After all, he grew up in Cleveland's West Side long before anyone had heard of Republic Powdered Metals. Over the years, as his company scaled the loftiest heights of corporate America, Sullivan kept in touch with the old neighborhood. He cajoled fellow executives to remember the West Side when they made their charitable contributions, which so often tended to flow to the trendier East Side. And his family continued to attend Saint Malachi Church in Cleveland's inner city. In the late 1980s, already curious about the Urban Community School, he met Sister Maureen.

"Saint Malachi's is located on the West Side of Cleveland," Sister Maureen explained. "It's in a neighborhood that struggles with all the consequences of poverty, where Saint Malachi's is a beacon of hope for many people who are homeless. I think Tom saw that. Tom saw that there is clearly outreach to people who are among the most needy in the greater Cleveland area, and he responded to that."

Unbeknownst to Sister Maureen, supporting the Urban Community School was also a chance to live up to a promise Sullivan had made to his wife, Sandy.

The Sullivans with Judy Collins at a dinner for the Ohio Cancer Research Associates at which Tom Sullivan was the honoree. From left to right are Tom Sullivan, Sandy Sullivan, Judy Collins, and Julie Sullivan.

"My mother was very involved in different organizations for the betterment of other folks," Sandy Sullivan explained. "I was always trying to get my hand in a little bit of this, and Tom was always saying, 'Hey, you have a huge responsibility with our family, and let's wait until our kids are grown. Then I promise you that I'll get involved along with you.'"

It was the sort of promise executives find easier to make than to keep. But Tom's father had taught that a Sullivan lives up to his word.

"I always thought that Tom got the best of my mother and father," said Kaki O'Neill, Tom's sister. "I was right. He not only excelled in the international business community, but also in his compelling generosity to those less fortunate, giving of his time and financial resources."

Sullivan eventually joined the board of the Urban Community School and began to apply his business acumen to the school's problems. Every year, the school struggled to raise enough money to make ends meet. It was a year-to-year existence. Sullivan spearheaded a fund-raising campaign to provide the school with an endowment, which initially raised $3.5 million. For the first time, the Urban Community School no longer existed hand-to-mouth, thanks to what Sister Maureen called Sullivan's "visionary approach."

"I'm convinced that one way to break the line of poverty is through education," said Sullivan. "Urban Community School not only gives these youngsters a great education but also teaches them faith, love, and respect. They won't all end up in college, but they'll all end up very productive citizens for this community."

Today the endowment stands at $9 million. That means that a lot more kids like Jose Gonzalez can be helped. Regarded as a model of urban education, the school is the first and only elementary school in Cleveland to receive the prestigious Excellence in Education Award from the U.S. Department of Education.

"I have to say he has fulfilled that promise to the Nth degree," Sandy Sullivan said. "He's really gotten involved and has done an awful lot, particularly for the near West Side of Cleveland."

Whatever happened to the shy little boy? Jose Gonzalez graduated from Notre Dame in 1991. After working at British Petroleum, Jose came back to teach at Urban Community School.

Encouraged by his wife Sandy, who had long since been involved with poverty issues on the near West Side of Cleveland, UCS is one of several organizations to benefit from Tom's efforts and financial support over the years.

The Malachi House, founded by Tom's sister Kaki and located on Cleveland's West Side, is another way the company gives back to its community. With significant support from RPM, the Malachi House provides a home for the terminally ill who are indigent.

transferred from Stonhard, where he had been CFO since the company's acquisition, to assume the position of RPM's CFO and take over leadership of the Purchasing Group. P. Kelly Tompkins replaced the retiring Paul A. Granzier as general counsel and corporate secretary.[6]

By 1998, forty people worked in the main office, more than twice as many as a few years before. Sheryl Redick, RPM's corporate receptionist, had been at the company for thirteen years and witnessed the growth firsthand. "The biggest change in RPM is the growth, the size of it," Redick said. "When I first started, I knew all the company names. I talked to every president. I knew a lot of the employees at the company by name, but now it's impossible to do that."[7]

But company sales had quadrupled during the same time, and the corporate staff was busier than ever before.[8] In 1998, RPM registered sales of $1.6 billion, a 20 percent single-year increase, and income of $149.6 million, a 10 percent increase.[9]

"For a company our size to have a staff of only forty people at corporate world headquarters is unheard of," said Kathie Rogers, director of investor relations. "But we all wear many hats. I was Jim Karman's assistant, but there was never a manager of investor relations per se. So when things came up with the shareholders or investors, I would just handle them. They gave me the title of manager of investor relations, which is something I've been learning about. But it's funny; when I got this promotion, everybody at corporate was like, 'Kathie, isn't that what you've been doing all along?'"[10]

As part of its move to bring its operating companies' marketing closer together, and to help its industrial customers, RPM announced in July 1999 that it was relaunching its Web site, www.rpminc.com. The upgraded site featured more information and enhanced capabilities.[11] Of the $60 million RPM invested in information technology in the late 1990s, $2.5 million went toward an Internet-based system that enabled customers to order on-line.[12] The overall effort was headed up by Vice President and Chief Information Officer Paul Hoogenboom, who hired ten additional people to form RPM's E-commerce Division.

Tom Sullivan Jr., who helped put together the Web site in addition to his duties running Tremco's international operation, said he wanted the site to extend his grandfather's tradition of using customer testimonials and case histories to sell RPM products. "I'm trying to get our salespeople in the field to go on-line and show different case histories and systems," Tom Sullivan said.[13]

The rest of RPM's information technology budget was designated for improved financial reporting.

Finally, along with this reorganization, RPM began to prepare for its third generation of leadership. In 1998, both Tom Sullivan and Jim Karman announced plans to retire in 2002. A year later, Jay Morris retired after more than twenty years as the chief corporate planner. But like his father before him, Tom Sullivan was blessed by the presence of a son. Frank C. Sullivan, already a senior executive and board member, was ready to move into the leadership position and was deeply involved in the company-wide restructuring.

At the Operating Level

RPM's broad restructuring was more than just an acknowledgment that the company had grown too large to be efficient. It was also a recognition that many of the large acquisition candidates had already been bought.[14] From then on, many of the acquisitions would be smaller investments handled lower down the ladder.[15]

The corporate office's job, then, would be to encourage the operating companies to pursue a broad, cohesive corporate acquisitions strategy.[16] This broadened responsibility was part of the rationale behind the expansion of the corporate staff.

Still, RPM's corporate leaders would likely never step away from acquisitions completely. In March 1998, RPM announced it was buying The Flecto Company for $67 million. Flecto, with annual sales of about $50 million, was a California company that made wood finishes under brand names such as Varathane and Watco. The company was purchased from John E. Vetterli, whose family had founded it in 1934.[17]

This move was followed by RPM's early 1999 repurchase of its 50 percent interest in Euclid Chemical from Holderbank Financiere Glaris of Switzerland.[18]

The operating companies, however, were more active. In 1998, Carboline completed the purchase of Nullifire, of Coventry, England, for $16 million. Nullifire boasted annual sales of about $15 million and made a line of fireproof coatings. Group Managing Director Nigel Maris stayed with Nullifire.[19] Seven additional acquisitions were negotiated in 1998 by RPM companies: Carboline Argentina/Tintas Letta; Carboline Europe/Corroline; Conica Technik; Ultra-Tex Surfaces; Prostruct; and Compositite. The string continued in 1999 and 2000 with Corrosion Services; Eucomex; Toxement Holderchem; Guardian Products; Epoxi-Tech; Agpro Limited; and Arr-Maz Products.

The DAP Acquisition

In 1999, however, RPM didn't stay out of the large-acquisition game completely. In July, the company announced the purchase of DAP Products from Wassall, a publicly traded British conglomer-ate, for $290 million in cash.[20] A very large consumer brand, DAP sold products under several names, including DAP, Durabond, and Weldwood. DAP's U.S.-based management, led by President and CEO John McLaughlin, planned to remain with RPM. "It will be business as usual," McLaughlin said.[21]

For RPM, however, the year was far from business as usual. DAP had excellent manufacturing capacity, which, in turn, increased RPM's overall manufacturing capacity beyond current needs. Moreover, RPM was still working through its own consolidation and, because of the size of the DAP acquisition, was forced to absorb a historically high level of company debt. Shortly after the acquisition, RPM announced a plan to rationalize its far-flung operations.

"As RPM has grown, we have come to recognize that consolidation of operating companies in similar businesses creates efficiencies," Sullivan said in 1999. "Building on the successful integration of Mameco and Republic Powdered Metals into our Tremco operation in fiscal 1998, we have initiated additional strategic consolidations."[22]

DAP's popular sealant and caulking. In 1999, RPM acquired DAP for $290 million, adding such well-known consumer brands as DAP, Durabond, and Weldwood.

Through its Rust-Oleum and DAP product lines, among others, RPM was able to offer stocking and management services to home improvement centers. Through the development of category management by the Rust-Oleum team, RPM companies became more important partners to their major retail customers.

These new consolidations took place within the existing two-division structure. In the Industrial Division, three new operating units were created:

- The StonCor Group, which combined the Stonhard, Carboline, Plasite Protective Coatings, and Fibergrate Composite Structures business units.
- The Tremco Group, which included Mameco, Republic Powdered Metals, and Euclid Chemical Company.
- The RPM II Group, which consisted of Dryvit, Day-Glo, American Emulsions, Alox, CHEMSPEC, TCI, Kop-Coat, and RPM/Belgium.

The Consumer Division comprised three operating units:

- The DAP Group.
- The Rust-Oleum Group.
- The Zinsser Group.

This reorganization went further than those of previous years. RPM was reducing its reporting units from more than twenty to six and was asking managers who had long managed only their own businesses to handle new product lines, manufacturing, and distribution. Moreover, this move was accompanied by a significant management reorganization and the closure of two offices, sixteen plants, and five warehouses. At the same time, about 10 percent of the company's workforce, or 730 jobs, would be eliminated.

In the 1999 annual report, Sullivan said, "In developing the consolidation program, it became apparent that, for the first time in its history, RPM should undergo a comprehensive restructuring of operations."[23]

In fiscal 2000, he said, RPM expected to take a significant restructuring charge.

The Millennium

This restructuring charge was not an easy pill to swallow. Heading into RPM's fifty-third year, management predicted that "in all likelihood, the special charge taken in fiscal 2000 will disrupt RPM's long-standing record of continuous per share earnings increases. However, we believe the program will set the stage for stronger earnings growth in the years ahead and represents a major investment in building long-term value for RPM shareholders."[24] Sales that year, however, were expected to set a new record, registering about $2 billion once the DAP acquisition started to take effect.

While RPM's management could predict trouble inside the company, they were caught unprepared in summer 1999 by sudden signs of weakness in the world's most robust economy. By this time, the United States was in its record eighth straight year of economic expansion. The boom was fueled by dramatically increased worker productivity, technology, dizzying stock market gains driven by Internet stocks, and runaway consumer confidence.

By summer 2000, however, certain sectors of the U.S. economy were beginning to soften. Technology stocks began a downward slide, dragging both major markets down with them. Then in April, oil prices skyrocketed, raising the cost of basic materials for chemical companies. The *Cleveland Plain Dealer* reported that this increase was hitting local chemical companies hard but RPM would probably be spared because of existing purchase agreements.[25]

That month, RPM issued its earnings report for the third quarter of fiscal 2000. Surprisingly, earnings were significantly lower than expected—not because of rising material costs but due to seasonally slower sales for DAP and unexpected costs associated with the restructuring. According to the *Plain Dealer*, RPM closed a StonCor corrosion plant, only to reopen it to fill existing orders. Similarly, there were problems with merging the wood finishes manufacturing operations.[26]

By the fourth quarter, with the plant closings and consolidations likely to stretch into the next year, Tom Sullivan knew the company was going to miss its earnings estimate of 87 cents per share. "I got surprised," he told the *Plain Dealer*, "and the analysts got surprised." Earnings, he said, would be closer to 73 cents per share—pushed further down by a higher-than-expected restructuring charge of $59.8 million.[27]

When the final figures were announced, RPM had indeed missed its earnings estimates. Sales rose to $1.95 billion, a 14 percent increase and a new sales record, but earnings were 73 cents per share, a 15 percent decline from the year before. RPM's consecutive streak of increased earnings had ended at fifty-two years.[28]

"It was a jolting year for us," Karman said. "But if some good comes out of it, which I think it will, we'll be in good shape."[29]

Following the announcement, newspapers across the country examined what had happened to America's longest streak of increasing company earnings. For RPM, part of the problem lay with earnings shortfalls in major product lines, including DAP, Testors, Bondo, and StonCor, and some more responsibility lay with the ongoing restructuring. It was clear that RPM had attempted too much at once, without anticipating the kinds of hiccups that occurred.

Beyond that, the analysts themselves shouldered part of the blame. In an era of sometimes irrational exuberance during a long growth streak, many U.S. stock analysts had become permanent optimists. Throughout 2000, earnings shortfall announcements became commonplace as companies like Proctor & Gamble and Goodyear all missed their forecasts. While not evading the issue,

Sullivan told a group of analysts that RPM had "tried to talk down over a period of time" some of the analysts' rosier predictions.[30]

Fortunately, as Sullivan had also predicted, the earnings situation was short-term. By the first quarter of 2001, RPM was able to announce robust earnings and a 12 percent increase in revenue over the previous year. At the company's annual meeting, directors approved a two percent increase in the quarterly dividend, its twenty-seventh consecutive increase.

Introspection

Even though RPM's financial condition began to improve, the company's stock price remained

Bondo was one of RPM's consumer products that enjoyed high visibility. The product had long been synonymous with car repair. In 2000, however, Bondo was one of the product lines that experienced earnings shortfalls.

depressed. There was considerable pressure on Tom Sullivan and Jim Karman to take further action. At the annual meeting in October, Tom Sullivan had found himself in the unusual position of confronting angry shareholders. "I answered three rather tough questions," he said.

> One was about the composition of our board of directors, which remains mostly a male board and mostly a white board. One had to do with the value of RPM shares, and obviously the restructuring and the fact that it wasn't done in the most efficient way. And the third thing I addressed was my salary and the bonus that was awarded to me last year in spite of the fact that it was a bad year.[31]

For each of these, Sullivan tried to answer as "honestly and effectively as possible," indicating that there probably had been too much tried too quickly. Regarding the stock price, he agreed but also pointed out restructuring had taken longer and cost more than expected. But he also pointed out that both the Nasdaq and the New York Stock Exchange were experiencing a correction that some-

After Tom Sullivan's election as chairman and CEO of the National Paint & Coatings Association, Jim Karman sent his friend a Western Union telegram congratulating him.

times wandered into bear territory. "We were going to take the hit regardless," he said.

Sullivan's salary was based on a formula that shareholders had voted on in 1997. In addition to a generous cash payment, the salary included options and the conversion of Sullivan's entire supplemental retirement fund into RPM stock instead of cash. On these last two items, Sullivan pointed out, his personal fortunes were directly tied to the performance of the company. "I have taken quite a hit," he said.[32]

For any CEO to answer questions like these is difficult. But for Tom Sullivan, who had taken a small family company with sales of around $11 million and transformed it into a $2 billion market leader, it was especially painful.

"We really initiated programs in the late 1990s," Tom Sullivan said. "One was the restructuring program, which involved closing several of our plants and downsizing by about 10 percent of our employees. The other was reorganizing the company into seven reporting groups."[33]

But part of their decision was motivated by the desire to leave RPM in good shape for Frank Sullivan. "Jim and I made this decision together," Sullivan said. "If we were going to leave, we'd rather give the ongoing management a clean slate rather than something that should be taken care of. We could have coasted, but had we coasted, I don't think the market would have been too much kinder to us."[34]

This decision earned the admiration of RPM's senior staff. After all, everyone was aware that Tom Sullivan could have retired with one of the best financial records of any CEO anywhere in corporate America. Instead, he chose to take on the tough task of restructuring, breaking the company's cherished record streak, and assuming full responsibility for the outcome.

"He didn't want to end up walking away with fifty-five years of records, and then someone the next year or two taking a big hit," said Dave Reif, president of the StonCor Group. "I think Tom wanted to let the new team get off to a fresh start. I think that's a good thing."[35]

The Plan

This degree of responsibility was something that, by 2001, had been hardwired into RPM's operating culture and the Sullivan family itself. The company had operated for thirty years—each of them a record year—by letting autonomous operating company presidents set their own goals, and then meet them. RPM's history has been the story of people entrusted to do their jobs well, to make smart and rational business decisions, and to consistently outperform even their own expectations. As Frank Sullivan said, "For the thirty years Tom Sullivan was at the helm, he's created success in a manner that has a whole lot more to do with trusting people and believing in them than with short-term profit and loss."[36]

It wasn't until RPM tried to break with its traditional operating structure—coupled with bad timing vis-á-vis the economy and stock markets—that it ran into trouble. Perhaps, as Tom Sullivan suggested, RPM should have brought in outside management consultants to help with such an ambitious reorganization. Perhaps, as Jim Karman frequently said, RPM had become "consumed with the process" and strayed from the fundamentals that made it successful for so long. Whatever the case, the management team going into summer 2001 was introspective and energetic at the same time, focused on regaining the company's momentum while continuing to adapt to its new form.

As a $2 billion company, RPM had become one of the largest paint and coatings companies in the world, operating as a much larger fish in a seemingly smaller pond. Every one of its movements sent exaggerated ripples through the investment community and its own industry, and RPM's leadership figured prominently in the business. In 2001, Tom Sullivan was elected chairman of the National Paint & Coating Association for a two-year term.

That June, RPM was once again looking forward to the future—but found that the challenges were not over yet. RPM emerged from its restructing into a U.S. economy that had continued to deteriorate, officially slipping into a recession in March. The once high-flying technology sector had been routed and manufacturing was depressed. Despite the general malaise, however, RPM was still upbeat. It was performing better than its competition and, even though

sales were expected to decline because of the divestiture of the Durabond unit of DAP, its earnings were at record highs. In his annual remarks to stockholders, Tom Sullivan said he expected a "love fest" at the annual meeting because of strong earnings.

"Obviously, we are seeing the benefit of our restructuring program, as well as lower interest rates," Sullivan said.[37]

RPM's Reorganization

RPM's reorganization into industrial and consumer divisions, each having three growth groups, was completed.

Mike Tellor, who joined RPM with the 1985 Carboline acquisition, was not the only individual to join RPM in an acquisition and go on to run a major growth platform. Indeed, that was a very successful pattern for RPM. By the turn of the century, Jeff Korach, who joined RPM in 1984 in the $7 million Euclid acquisition, became president of the $400 million Tremco Group; Bob Senior, who joined RPM in 1987 in the $25 million Zinsser acquisition, became the president of the $200 million Zinsser Group; Chuck Pauli, who joined RPM in 1990 in the $54 million Kop-Coat acquisition, went on to be president of the $300 million RPM II Group; and Dave Reif, who joined RPM in the 1994, $100 million Stonhard acquisition, went on to become president of the $400 million StonCor Group.

This is an outstanding example of RPM following the original philosophy handed down by its founder, Frank Sullivan. No other company in the industry has been able to attract top managers through an acquisition program, create the atmosphere to keep them and continue to promote them into more meaningful jobs.

Yet this speech to shareholders, delivered on October 12, 2001, was delivered against the backdrop of a national tragedy. On September 11, 2001, terrorists hijacked four passenger aircraft with the intention of destroying American landmarks. As a result of these attacks, the World Trade Center in New York City was destroyed, as was part of the Pentagon outside Washington, D.C. The fourth plane crashed in rural Pennsylvania after passengers overcame the terrorists. The effect of these attacks was tremendous. Almost three thousand people lost their lives, the national economy, which was still limping through

a recession, declined sharply, and the United States launched a global war against terrorism.

When he heard about the attacks, Tom Sullivan was in Europe, scouting out new acquisitions and "doing business-wise what I love the most—trying to sell other companies on joining RPM." As he watched the horror unfold, Sullivan sat in his hotel room and drew up a list of what was important in his life. That list included his faith, his family, and his friends. Significantly, RPM's short-term stock fluctuation was nowhere to be seen.

"Don't get me wrong," he told shareholders.

I fully understand my duties and responsibilities as CEO of a publicly owned company, and certainly one of the major ones is to return value to shareholders, as well as give value to our employees, our companies, and our customers. In doing so, you have to look beyond the immediate quarter or sometimes the given year. The past two fiscal years for RPM are a good example of this. We could have

easily slid past the last two years doing nothing and probably posted our fifty-third and fifty-fourth consecutive record years in earnings and earnings per share.... Jim Karman and I chose not to do that. We had a massive restructuring, we organized our business, and we developed an excellent management team headed by Frank Sullivan.[38]

Indeed, the focus on RPM was increasingly shifting to Frank Sullivan, which was only logical. In early 2002, after RPM hit record earnings on essentially flat sales and the stock was rising once again, Tom Sullivan and Jim Karman planned to go ahead with their retirements later that year. The financial press and analyst community began to anticipate Frank Sullivan's leadership—and found that he was ready.

"One of the important things about RPM's recent strategic plan is that it actually bridges this management succession," Ken Evans said. "Frank is a very bright guy. He had virtually grown up in RPM.

Opposite: RPM's operating presidents in 2002. From left to right are Mike Tellor; John McLaughlin; Bob Senior; Chuck Pauli; Jeff Korach; and Dave Reif.

Below:The RPM corporate officers in 2002. From left to right, standing, are Dennis Finn, vice president of environmental and regulatory affairs; Robert Matejka, chief financial officer; Frank Sullivan, president; Ronald Rice, vice president, administration; Stephen Knoop, vice president, corporate development; Glenn Hasman, vice president, finance and communications; Keith Smiley, vice president and treasurer; from left to right seated are P. Kelly Tompkins, vice president, general counsel, and secretary; and Paul Hoogenboom, vice president, operations and systems.

He's fully trusted by Tom and very respected by the organization."[39]

In early 2002, *InsideBusiness* magazine ran a feature story on the third Sullivan to run RPM. "The younger Sullivan adheres to the founder's core belief," wrote reporter Michael Zawacki. "'Hire the best people you can find. Create an atmosphere that will keep them. Then let them do their jobs.'"[40]

Frank made it clear that he intended to uphold RPM's traditions in a variety of ways. Not only did he pass out photos of his grandfather in 1970 posing next to a car with vanity plates that read 168, he also announced the ambitious goal to double RPM's size in five years. This would mean an astronomical jump in sales from $2 billion to $4 billion. With single-digit

growth expected in RPM's operating companies, this means significant acquisition activity. For Frank, it also means keeping alive a legacy of excellence that extends far beyond the bottom line.

"The financial side, to me, is the scorecard that determines whether the real business principles are the right ones and are successful," he said. "My role as CEO is to deliver shareholder value. But it's to deliver shareholder value in the long term."[41]

The best way to do this, Frank said, is to maintain the company's culture while adapting to its new form.

"My father likes to tell people that he was sandwiched between two Frank Sullivans—his father and his son," said Frank.

But if you look at the history of RPM, I have every reason to believe that we'll be marvelously successful in the future because we've got a great base of business, great people, and great momentum.

My grandfather started the business, but the guy who put it on the map was my father, and now we've got a great team in place that will keep this

company successful. I think that there are two Frank Sullivans that are pretty lucky they were on either end of Tom Sullivan.[42]

By the end of the 2002 fiscal year, on May 31, 2002, RPM completed its restructuring program, reorganized to achieve multi-billion dollar growth in the future, and reduced its debt-to-capital ratio to 45 percent.

Over the years, it aquired some of the most respected brands in the industrial and consumer markets. Most importantly, throughout the late 1990s, RPM developed an outstanding management team, both at the corporate and operating level, to move RPM forward in its next growth phase.

RPM's board of directors in 2002. Seated left to right are Dr. Jerry Sue Thornton and Lorrie Gustin. Standing left to right are Donald Miller, Bill Papenbrock, Edward Brandon, Frank Sullivan, Jim Karman, E. Bradley Jones, Albert Ratner, Tom Sullivan, Joe Viviano, and Dr. Max D. Amstutz.

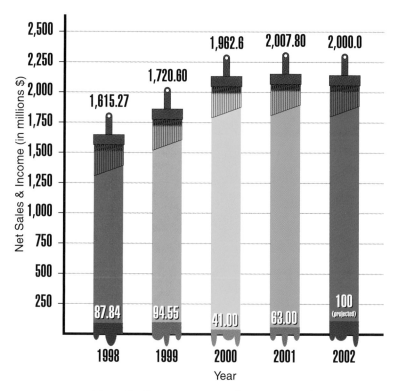

Above: Frank and Tom Sullivan in 2001. By 2002, with Frank Sullivan leading the company, Tom Sullivan was looking forward to his October retirement.

Left: RPM's sales and earning for 1998 through 2002 (projected). Earnings are represented by the darker area within the sales bar.

Tom Sullivan was ready to pass the baton.

In their last letter to RPM shareholders, Tom and Jim wrote:

We have been both humbled and gratified to preside over the growth of a small, single line, specialty coatings business into a $2 billion global leader in specialty coatings. During the past 30 years, RPM has become home for companies and brands that lead in our field, and it has been our distinct pleasure to work with the people behind them.

Beyond our legacy of helping to grow RPM over the past several decades, we feel the most important contribution we could make to long-term shareholder value is to conduct an orderly transition of management to a new team capable of growing the business well beyond where it is today. We are extremely proud of this management group that has been assembled and are pleased to introduce these individuals to you in this, our last annual report as executive officers of RPM, Inc.

As RPM grew and prospered, we felt it important that the company contribute to the betterment of our community, and we are proud of RPM's record in corporate citizenship. We fully expect that the company will continue to exercise its responsibility to its communities.

We are extremely appreciative of the support we have received over the years from the professional investment community, individual and institutional shareholders, employees, customers, and suppliers. We are especially indebted to the extended Sullivan and Karman families for their kindnesses and loyalty during our tenure. We look forward to continuing with RPM in advisory capacities, and have every confidence that the new management team will eclipse the accomplishments of the old.

NOTES TO SOURCES

Chapter One

1. Thomas Sullivan, *To Frank Sullivan* (Cleveland: RPM, Inc., 1971), 1.

2. Thomas Sullivan, *To Frank Sullivan* (Cleveland: RPM, Inc., 1971), 1.

3. Charles Sullivan, interviewed by Jay Miller and David Patten, tape recording, 31 August 2000, Write Stuff Enterprises.

4. Charles Sullivan, interviewed by Jay Miller and David Patten, tape recording, 31 August 2000, Write Stuff Enterprises.

5. George Heckel, *The Paint Industry: Reminiscences and Comments* (St. Louis; American Paint Journal Co., 1931), 302.

6. Fred Schulenberg, "Cleveland (Pt. 1): Not just great, but the greatest," *American Paint and Coatings Journal*, 5 January 1987, 39.

7. Harland Hatcher, *The Western Reserve: The Story of New Connecticut in Ohio*, 2nd ed. (Cleveland: The World Publishing Co., 1966) 218.

8. Fred Schulenberg, "Cleveland (Pt. 1): Not just great, but the greatest," *American Paint and Coatings Journal*, 5 January 1987, 39.

9. "Sells Contents of House," *Cleveland Press*, 9 May 1957.

10. Thomas Sullivan, *To Frank Sullivan* (Cleveland: RPM, Inc., 1971), 1.

11. Thomas Sullivan, *To Frank Sullivan* (Cleveland: RPM, Inc., 1971), 1.

12. David D. Van Tassell and John J. Grabowski, eds., *The Encyclopedia of Cleveland History*, 2nd ed. (Bloomington and Indianapolis, Indiana: Indiana University Press, 1996), 38.

13. William Ganson Rose, *Cleveland: The Making of a City* (Cleveland and New York: World

Publishing Co., 1950), 810.

14. Thomas Sullivan, *To Frank Sullivan* (Cleveland: RPM, Inc., 1971).

15. Robert D. Deitz, interviewed by David Patten, tape recording, 30 August 2000, Write Stuff Enterprises.

16. Thomas Sullivan, *To Frank Sullivan* (Cleveland: RPM, Inc., 1971).

17. Thomas Sullivan, *To Frank Sullivan* (Cleveland: RPM, Inc., 1971).

18. Sue Jacobus, interviewed by David Patten, tape recording, 8 October 2000, Write Stuff Enterprises.

19. Sue Jacobus, interviewed by David Patten, tape recording, 8 October 2000, Write Stuff Enterprises.

20. Robert F. Fleming, interviewed by David Patten, tape recording, 31 August 2000, Write Stuff Enterprises.

21. Thomas Sullivan, *To Frank Sullivan* (Cleveland: RPM, Inc., 1971).

22. Charles Sullivan, interviewed by Jay Miller and David Patten, tape recording, 31 August 2000, Write Stuff Enterprises.

23. David D. Van Tassell and John J. Grabowski, eds., *The Encyclopedia of Cleveland History,* 2nd ed. (Bloomington and Indianapolis, Indiana: Indiana University Press, 1996), 38.

24. Fred Schulenberg, "Cleveland (Pt. 1): Not just great, but the greatest," *American Paint and Coatings Journal,* 5 January 1987, 39.

25. Fred Schulenberg, "Cleveland (Pt. 1): Not just great, but the greatest," *American Paint and Coatings Journal,* 5 January 1987, 39.

26. Larry Anderson, "Watching Closely as an Industry Grows Up," *Modern Paint and Coatings,* July 1996, 18.

27. Thomas Sullivan, *To Frank Sullivan* (Cleveland: RPM, Inc., 1971).

28. Acorn Refining Co. sales bulletin, 19 February 1942, RPM archives.

29. Julius K. Nemeth, interviewed by David Patten, tape recording, 9 October 2000, Write Stuff Enterprises.

30. Robert F. Fleming, interviewed by David Patten, tape recording, 31 August 2000, Write Stuff Enterprises.

31. Julius K. Nemeth, interviewed by David Patten, tape recording, 9 October 2000, Write Stuff Enterprises.

32. Sue Jacobus, interviewed by David Patten, 8 October 2000, tape recording, Write Stuff Enterprises.

33. Joan Livingston, interviewed by Jon VanZile, tape recording, 11 April 2002, Write Stuff Enterprises.

34. Thomas Sullivan, *To Frank Sullivan* (Cleveland: RPM, Inc., 1971), 1.

35. Thomas Sullivan, correspondence to Jon VanZile, 7 April 2002, Write Stuff Enterprises.

36. Marilyn Brace, interviewed by David Patten, tape recording, 2 February 2002, Write Stuff Enterprises.

37. Randall E. Pelton, "RPM is buying companies again," *Ohio Business*, December 1984.

38. Thomas Sullivan, *To Frank Sullivan* (Cleveland: RPM, Inc., 1971).

39. Republic Powdered Metals Inc., Prospectus, 16 November 1963, 6.

40. Julius K. Nemeth, interviewed by David Patten, tape recording, 9 October 2000, Write Stuff Enterprises.

41. Thomas Sullivan, interviewed by David Patten, tape recording, 31 August 2000, Write Stuff Enterprises.

42. Robert F. Fleming, interviewed by David Patten, tape recording, 31 August 2000, Write Stuff Enterprises.

43. RPM, Inc., 1977 Annual Report, 7.

44. Robert F. Fleming, interviewed by David Patten, tape recording, 31 August 2000, Write Stuff Enterprises.

45. "Summer Slumps Can Be Avoided," *Electrical Production*, April 1955, 16.

46. "Summer Slumps Can Be Avoided," *Electrical Production*, April 1955, 16.

47. Julius K. Nemeth, interviewed by David Patten, tape recording, 9 October 2000, Write Stuff Enterprises.

48. Frank A. Cartile, correspondence to Frank C. Sullivan, 27 April 1953.

49. Jack Cleary, "Foregoes Security: Builds $2 Million Sales in Five Years," *Cleveland News*, 20 June 1955.

50. Jack Cleary, "Foregoes Security: Builds $2 Million Sales in Five

Years," *Cleveland News*, 20 June 1955.

51. Frank C. Sullivan, correspondence to Joe Ciulla, 13 June 1967, RPM archives.

52. Thomas Sullivan, *To Frank Sullivan* (Cleveland: RPM, Inc., 1971), 62.

53. Robert F. Fleming, interviewed by David Patten, tape recording, 31 August 2000, Write Stuff Enterprises.

54. Commander R. C. Benitez, correspondence to Republic Powdered Metals, undated.

55. Malaquias Peréz Miguel Alcolado Arquitectos, correspondence to Republic Powdered Metals, 19 August 1958.

56. Thomas Sullivan, *To Frank Sullivan* (Cleveland: RPM, Inc., 1971).

57. "An Invitation from Republic Powered Metals," brochure, 1963, RPM archives.

58. Fred McGunagle, "Firm Donates $500 to

Promote City Port," 11 September 1962.

59. Joe Ciulla, interviewed by David Patten, tape recording, 7 November 2000, Write Stuff Enterprises.

60. Joe Ciulla, interviewed by David Patten, tape recording, 7 November 2000, Write Stuff Enterprises.

61. Robert F. Fleming, interviewed by David Patten, tape recording, 31 August 2000, Write Stuff Enterprises.

62. Thomas Sullivan, *To Frank Sullivan* (Cleveland: RPM, Inc., 1971).

63. Republic Powdered Metals Inc., Prospectus, 16 November 1963, 7.

64. "Irish Eyes That Smiled," *Ohio Thoroughbred*, October 1971.

65. Mary Ann Peterman, interviewed by David Patten, tape recording, 31 August 2000, Write Stuff Enterprises.

66. Isi Newborn, "Sullivan's death is a loss to Thoroughbred racing," *The Cleveland Press*, 20 August 1971.

67. Isi Newborn, "Sullivan's death is a loss to Thoroughbred racing," *The Cleveland Press*, 20 August 1971.

68. Isi Newborn, "Sullivan's death is a loss to Thoroughbred racing," *The Cleveland Press*, 20 August 1971.

69. Robert F. Fleming, interviewed by David Patten, tape recording, 31 August 2000, Write Stuff Enterprises.

70. Robert F. Fleming, interviewed by David Patten, tape recording, 31 August 2000, Write Stuff Enterprises.

71. John Mars, interviewed by David Patten, tape recording, 9 February 2001, Write Stuff Enterprises.

72. Sandra Sullivan, interviewed by David Patten, tape recording, 31 August 2000, Write Stuff Enterprises.

73. Thomas Sullivan, interviewed by David Patten, tape recording, 7 November 2000, Write Stuff Enterprises.

74. Jim Karman, interviewed by David Patten, tape recording, 30 August 2000, Write Stuff Enterprises.

Chapter Two

1. Thomas Sullivan, interviewed by David Patten, tape recording, 31 August 2000, Write Stuff Enterprises.

2. Julius K. Nemeth, interviewed by David Patten, tape recording, 9 October 2000, Write Stuff Enterprises.

3. Frank C. Sullivan, correspondence to Joe Ciulla, 13 June 1967, RPM archives.

4. Thomas Sullivan, interviewed by David Patten, tape recording, 31 August 2000, Write Stuff Enterprises.

5. Robert F. Fleming, interviewed by David

Patten, tape recording, 31 August 2000, Write Stuff Enterprises.

6. Rudy Zappi, "Republic Powdered Metals Firm Plans Move to Brunswick Hills," *Cleveland Press*, 5 August 1963.

7. Sam Boyer, "Brunswick Hills Industry Unusual," *Medina County Gazette*

8. Marilyn Brace, interviewed by David Patten, tape recording, 2 February 2002, Write Stuff Enterprises.

9. *The Kline Guide to the Paint Industry*, 4th ed. (New York: Charles H. Kline & Company, 1965).

10. *The Kline Guide to the Paint Industry*, Fourth ed. (New York: Charles H. Kline & Company, 1965).

11. Jim Karman, interviewed by David Patten, tape recording, 30 September 2000, Write Stuff Enterprises.

12. Thomas Sullivan, "30 Years of Acquisitions,"

13. Thomas Sullivan, "The Fun and Challenge from $3 Million to $600 Million," speech to students at Case Western Reserve University, 26 February 1993, 14.

14. Sam Boyer, "RPM's Business Is Booming," *Medina County Gazette*, 29 July 1971, 12.

15. John J. Cleary, "Powdered Metals Buys Reardon Co.," *Cleveland Plain Dealer*, 25 February 1966.

16. "The Reardon Co. to Be Sold," *St. Louis Post-Dispatch*, 24 February 1966.

17. "The Reardon Co. to Be Sold," *St. Louis Post-Dispatch*, 24 February 1966.

18. "Closing Agenda for purchase of assets of The Reardon Company," undated, RPM archives.

19. Thomas Sullivan, "The Fun and Challenge from $3 Million to $600

Million," speech to students at Case Western Reserve University, 26 February 1993, 14.

20. Thomas Sullivan, interviewed by David Patten, tape recording, 31 August 2000, Write Stuff Enterprises.

21. Thomas Sullivan, interviewed by David Patten, tape recording, 20 September 2000, Write Stuff Enterprises.

22. Thomas Sullivan, interviewed by David Patten, tape recording, 31 August 2000, Write Stuff Enterprises.

23. Sandra Sullivan, interviewed by David Patten, tape recording, 31 August 2000, Write Stuff Enterprises.

24. Thomas Sullivan, "The Fun and Challenge from $3 Million to $600 Million," speech to students at Case Western Reserve University, 26 February 1993, 14.

25. Julius K. Nemeth, interviewed by David

Patten, tape recording, 9 October 2000, Write Stuff Enterprises.

26. RPM, Inc., 1968 Annual Report.

27. RPM, Inc., 1973 Annual Report.

28. Jim Karman, interviewed by David Patten, tape recording, 30 August 2000, Write Stuff Enterprises.

29. "RPM Has Acquired a Paint Company," *Medina County Gazette*, 14 October 1970,

30. Joe Ciulla, interviewed by David Patten, tape recording, 7 November 2000, Write Stuff Enterprises.

31. Thomas Sullivan, "30 Years of Acquisitions," undated speech, RPM archives.

32. "Pierce Co. Acquired by Brunswick's RPM," *Medina County Gazette*, 12 July 1971.

33. Thomas Sullivan, "The Fun and Challenge from $3 Million to $600 Million," speech to students at Case

Western Reserve University, 26 February 1993, 14.

34. RPM, Inc., 1969 Annual Report.

35. William Papenbrock, interviewed by David Patten, tape recording, 8 November 2000, Write Stuff Enterprises.

36. William Papenbrock, interviewed by David Patten, tape recording, 8 November 2000, Write Stuff Enterprises.

37. RPM, Inc., 1969 Annual Report.

Chapter Three

1. Charles Sullivan interview.

2. Noreen Wendt, interviewed by Jay Miller, tape recording, 31 August 2000, Write Stuff Enterprises.

3. Joan Livingston, interviewed by Jon VanZile, tape recording, 11 April 2002, Write Stuff Enterprises.

4. Noreen Wendt, interviewed by Jay

Miller, tape recording, 31 August 2000, Write Stuff Enterprises.

5. Sue Jacobus, interviewed by David Patten, 8 October 2000, tape recording, Write Stuff Enterprises.

6. Thomas Sullivan, interviewed by David Patten, tape recording, 20 September 2000, Write Stuff Enterprises.

7. Bob Batchelor, "Full RPM," *Inside Business*, October 1999, 68–69.

8. Mike Moore, "Even when economy is off RPM keeps rolling along," *The Cleveland Press*, 25 January 1971.

9. RPM, Inc., 1970 Annual Report.

10. Sam Boyer, "Highest Excellence Award Goes to Brunswick RPM," *Medina County Gazette*, 23 May 1970.

11. RPM, Inc., 1971 Annual Report.

12. RPM, Inc., 1971 Annual Report.

13. RPM, Inc., 1972 Annual Report.

14. RPM, Inc., 1971 Annual Report.
15. RPM, Inc., 1971 Annual Report.
16. RPM, Inc., 1972 Annual Report.
17. Thomas Sullivan, interviewed by David Patten, tape recording, 20 September 2000, Write Stuff Enteprises.
18. Thomas Sullivan, interviewed by David Patten, tape recording, 20 September 2000, Write Stuff Enteprises.
19. Thomas Sullivan, correspondence to Jon VanZile, 7 April 2002, Write Stuff Enterprises.
20. Thomas Sullivan, interviewed by David Patten, tape recording, 20 September 2000, Write Stuff Enteprises.
21. Thomas Sullivan, interviewed by David Patten, tape recording, 20 September 2000, Write Stuff Enteprises.
22. RPM, Inc., 1973 Annual Report.
23. RPM, Inc., 1973 Annual Report.
24. RPM, Inc., 1974 Annual Report, 3.
25. "Thibaut Purchased by RPM," *American Paint and Wall Coverings Dealer*, April 1976, 45.
26. "RPM Acquires Wallpaper Distributor," *CAC Journal*, April 1976, 26–27.
27. RPM, Inc., 1976 Annual Report.
28. "Broad Mix of Protective Coatings Adds Luster to Results of RPM," *Barron's*, 28 July 1975, 26.
29. "RPM expects 30th record growth year," *(Cleveland) Plain Dealer*, 24 July 1976.
30. Bob Batchelor, "Full RPM," *Inside Business*, October 1999, 68–69.

Chapter Four

1. Thomas Sullivan, "The Fun and Challenge from $3 Million to $600 Million," speech to students at Case Western Reserve University, 26 February 1993, 14.
2. Jim Karman, interviewed by David Patten, tape recording, 30 August 2000, Write Stuff Enterprises.
3. "Investment club advised of TransOhio advantages," *(Cleveland) Plain Dealer*, 21 January 1976.
4. "A Stock to Study," *Better Investing*, December 1976.
5. "Broad Mix of Protective Coatings Adds Luster to Results of RPM," *Barron's*, 28 July 1975, 26.
6. "RPM, Inc., Votes 50% Stock Payout; Net Up Again in Aug. 31 Period," *Northern Ohio Business Journal*, 3 October 1977.
7. RPM, Inc., 1976 Annual Report, 1.
8. Jim Karman, interviewed by David Patten, tape recording, 30 August 2000, Write Stuff Enterprises.
9. "RPM to build $250,000 office building," *Medina Gazette*, 26 November 1976.

10. "RPM Headquarters ... A Showcase for Company Products," *American Paint & Coatings Journal*, 17 April 1978, 58.

11. "RPM, Inc., is its own living ad in new Medina offices," *Northern Ohio Business Journal*, 14 November 1977, 12.

12. Mary Hall Crawford, interviewed by David Patten, tape recording, 30 August 2000, Write Stuff Enterprises.

13. "Hobby Paint Firm Relocates in Amsterdam," *Gloversville (N.Y.) Leader-Herald*, 20 May 1976.

14. Jim Karman, interviewed by David Patten, tape recording, 30 August 2000, Write Stuff Enterprises.

15. Jim Karman, interviewed by David Patten, tape recording, 30 August 2000, Write Stuff Enterprises.

16. Jay Morris, interviewed by David Patten, tape recording, 30 August 2000, Write Stuff Enterprises.

17. Jeffrey Bendix, "RPM Stirs It Up," *Cleveland Enterprise*, summer 1992, 22.

18. Jay Morris, interviewed by David Patten, tape recording, 30 August 2000, Write Stuff Enterprises.

19. Jay Morris, interviewed by David Patten, tape recording, 30 August 2000, Write Stuff Enterprises.

20. Jay Morris, interviewed by David Patten, tape recording, 30 August 2000, Write Stuff Enterprises.

21. Thomas Sullivan, interviewed by David Patten, tape recording, 20 September 2000, Write Stuff Enteprises.

22. Jay Morris, interviewed by David Patten, tape recording, 30 August 2000, Write Stuff Enterprises.

23. Jay Morris, interviewed by David Patten, tape recording, 30 August 2000, Write Stuff Enterprises.

24. Jeffrey Bendix, "RPM Stirs It Up," *Cleveland Enterprise*, summer 1992, 22.

25. Jay Morris, interviewed by David Patten, tape recording, 30 August 2000, Write Stuff Enterprises.

26. Jay Morris, interviewed by David Patten, tape recording, 30 August 2000, Write Stuff Enterprises.

27. Jay Morris, interviewed by David Patten, tape recording, 30 August 2000, Write Stuff Enterprises.

28. Jay Morris, interviewed by David Patten, 30 August 2000, tape recording, Write Stuff Enterprises.

29. Jay Morris, interviewed by David Patten, 30 August 2000, tape recording, Write Stuff Enterprises.

30. Jay Morris, interviewed by David Patten, 30 August 2000, tape recording, Write Stuff Enterprises.

31. Jay Morris, interviewed by David Patten, 30 August 2000, tape recording, Write Stuff Enterprises.

32. Victoria Harrow, "Paint by Number," *Small Business News Cleveland*, March 1999.

33. Jeffrey Bendix, "RPM Stirs it up," *Cleveland Enterprise*, Summer 1992, 26.

34. Robert D. Deitz, interviewed by David Patten, tape recording, 30 August 2000, Write Stuff Enterprises.

35. Charles G. Pauli, interviewed by David Patten, tape recording, 31 August 2000, Write Stuff Enterprises.

36. Jay Morris, interviewed by David Patten, 30 August 2000, tape recording, Write Stuff Enterprises.

37. Jay Morris, interviewed by David Patten, 30 August 2000, tape recording, Write Stuff Enterprises.

38. RPM, Inc., 1976 Annual Report, 1.

39. RPM, Inc., 1977 Annual Report, 2.

40. RPM, Inc., 1978 Annual Report, 5.

41. RPM, Inc., 1979 Annual Report, 3.

42. Fred Schulenberg, "Part VI: And the list goes on and on," *American Paint and Coatings Journal*, 16 March 1987, 37.

43. "RPM, Inc., Acquires Alox Corporation," *American Paint and Coatings Journal*, 22 August 1977.

44. "Maharam Fabric Is Acquired by RPM," *Northern Ohio Business Journal*, 31 October 1977.

45. Jim Karman, interviewed by David Patten, tape recording, 20 February 2001, Write Stuff Enterprises.

46. Thomas Sullivan, correspondence to Jon VanZile, 8 April 2002, Write Stuff Enterprises.

47. Thomas Sullivan, interviewed by David Patten, tape recording, 20 September 2000, Write Stuff Enteprises.

48. RPM, Inc., 1977 Annual Report, 4.

49. "RPM's Up Again," *Chemical Progress*, November 1978, 3.

50. RPM, Inc., 1977 Annual Report, 4–10.

51. John Leo Koshar, "Burgeoning RPM reorganizes," *(Cleveland) Plain Dealer*, 30 September 1978, 4D.

52. "RPM Acquires Mameco International, Producer of Sealants, Specialties," *American Paint & Coatings Journal*, 12 March 1979, 62.

53. Jim Karman, interviewed by David Patten, tape recording, 20 February 2001, Write Stuff Enterprises.

54. RPM, Inc., 1980 Annual Report, 3.

55. "RPM Acquires Mameco International, Producer of Sealants, Specialties," *American Paint & Coatings Journal*, 12 March 1979, 62.

56. RPM, Inc., 1980 Annual Report, 3.

57. David Prizinsky, "RPM defying recession; sales may pass $500 million," *Crain's Cleveland Business*, 4 March 1991, 4.

Chapter Five

1. Thomas Sullivan, "30 Years of Acquisitions," undated speech, RPM archives.

2. Victoria Harrow, "Paint by Number," *Small Business News Cleveland*, March 1999.

3. RPM, Inc., 1980 Annual Report, 3.

4. Robert Grace, "RPM inks joint venture to build polyisobutylene plant in North Carolina," *Rubber & Plastics News*, 10 August 1981, 1.

5. Victoria Harrow, "Paint by Number," *Small Business News Cleveland*, March 1999.

6. Delinda Karle, "Rebounding RPM prunes lagging operations," *Crain's Cleveland Business*, 26 October 1981, 17.

7. "RPM is seeking 34th year of record profit," *Akron Beacon Journal*, 9 September 1980.

8. RPM, Inc., 1982 Annual Report, 8.

9. RPM, Inc., 1982 Annual Report, 2.

10. RPM, Inc., 1980 Annual Report, 3.

11. Robert Grace, "RPM inks joint venture to build polyisobutylene plant in North Carolina," *Rubber & Plastics News*, 10 August 1981, 1.

12. W. Wesley Howard III, "RPM aims at key markets, expects continued growth," *Crain's Cleveland Business*, 13 October 1980, 16.

13. Doug Oplinger, "Rubber reshapes roof business," *Akron Beacon Journal*, 14 May 1984, B1.

14. RPM, Inc., 1982 Annual Report, 21.

15. "RPM keeps expanding, buys Haartz-Mason," *Rubber and Plastics News*, 29 September 1980, 14.

16. Press release, RPM, Inc., 15 September 1980.

17. "RPM keeps expanding, buys Haartz-Mason," *Rubber and Plastics News*, 29 September 1980, 14.

18. Robert Grace, "RPM inks joint venture to build polyisobutylene plant in North Carolina," *Rubber & Plastics News*, 10 August 1981, 1.

19. Delinda Karle, "Rebounding RPM prunes lagging operations," *Crain's Cleveland Business*, 26 October 1981, 17.

20. Bradley Hitchings, "Selling Your Small Company," *Business Week*, 4 February 1985, 85.

21. Bradley Hitchings, "Selling Your Small Company," *Business Week*, 4 February 1985, 85.

22. RPM, Inc., 1983 Annual Report, 2.

23. Randall Pelton, "RPM is getting ready to grow,"

Medina County Gazette, 14 October 1983.

24. "Dividend Achievers Suffer First Setback," *Dun's Business Month,* December 1983, 121.

25. The Beardstown Ladies Investment Club with Leslie Whitaker, *The Beardstown Ladies Common-Sense Investment Guide* (New York: Hyperion, 1994), 116.

26. "RPM, Inc. acquires firm that produces model glue," *(Cleveland) Plain Dealer,* 18 January 1984.

27. "RPM, Inc. buys Testor, maker of hobby paints," *Medina County Gazette,* 18 January 1984.

28. "Testor History," www.testor.com.

29. "RPM, Inc. buys Testor, maker of hobby paints," *Medina County Gazette,* 18 January 1984.

30. "RPM purchases Euclid Chemical," *Crain's Cleveland Business,* 13 August 1984.

31. Jay Miller, "Euclid Chemical pins high hopes on fast-setting concrete formula," *Crain's Cleveland Business,* 14 June 1982, 15.

32. Jeffrey Korach, interviewed by David Patten, tape recording, 8 November 2000, Write Stuff Enterprises.

33. "Company info," www.euclidchemical. com.

34. Frank Sullivan II, interviewed by David Patten, tape recording, 8 November 2000, Write Stuff Enterprises.

35. Frank Sullivan II, interviewed by David Patten, tape recording, 8 November 2000, Write Stuff Enterprises.

36. Frank Sullivan II, interviewed by David Patten, tape recording, 8 November 2000, Write Stuff Enterprises.

37. Sandra Sullivan, interviewed by David Patten, tape recording, 31 August 2000, Write Stuff Enterprises.

Chapter Six

1. *Value Line Investment Survey,* 22 February 1985.

2. Pamela Russell, "RPM Sees Further Growth in '85," *Investor's Daily,* 23 January 1985.

3. "RPM purchases maker of protective coatings," *Akron Beacon Journal,* 31 January 1985.

4. Pamela Russell, "RPM Sees Further Growth in '85," *Investor's Daily,* 23 January 1985.

5. Randall E. Pelton, "RPM Is Buying Companies— Again," *Ohio Business,* December 1984.

6. "RPM: Say It Ain't So, Tom," *OTC Review,* September 1985, 8.

7. William C. Roney III, "Progress Report—RPM," Roney & Co., 8 April 1985.

8. RPM, Inc., 1985 Annual Report, 2.

9. Press release, Sun Co., 1 October 1985, RPM archives.

10. Thomas Sullivan, interviewed by David Patten, tape recording, 31 August 2000, Write Stuff Enterprises.

11. Mike Tellor, interviewed by David Patten, tape recording, 7 November 2000, Write Stuff Enterprises.

12. Thomas Sullivan, interviewed by David Patten, tape recording, 31 August 2000, Write Stuff Enterprises.

13. Thomas Sullivan, interviewed by David Patten, tape recording, 31 August 2000, Write Stuff Enterprises.

14. Thomas Sullivan, interviewed by David Patten, tape recording, 31 August 2000, Write Stuff Enterprises.

15. Thomas Sullivan, interviewed by David Patten, tape recording, 31 August 2000, Write Stuff Enterprises.

16. Thomas Sullivan, interviewed by David S. Patten, tape recording, 31 August 2000, Write Stuff Enterprises.

17. Thomas Sullivan, interviewed by David Patten, tape recording, 31 August 2000, Write Stuff Enterprises.

18. Thomas Sullivan, interviewed by David Patten, tape recording, 31 August 2000, Write Stuff Enterprises.

19. Doug Oplinger, "RPM moves to pay for Carboline purchase," *Akron Beacon Journal*, 9 October 1985.

20. Mike Tellor, interviewed by David Patten, tape recording, 7 November 2000, Write Stuff Enterprises.

21. James M. Arenson, Donaldson, Lufkin & Jenrette action recommendation, 12 November 1985, 2–8.

22. Mike Tellor, interviewed by David Patten, tape recording, 7 November 2000, Write Stuff Enterprises.

23. Doug Oplinger, "RPM moves to pay for Carboline purchase," *Akron Beacon Journal*, 9 October 1985.

24. RPM, Inc., 1986 Annual Report, 3.

25. "RPM, Inc.'s Winning Strategy," *Merger Management Report*, September 1986.

26. "RPM, Inc., acquires PCI Industries, Inc.," *American Paint & Coatings Journal*, 14 July 1986, 12.

27. Michael Selz, "RPM Bases Success on Keeping Owners of Firms It Buys—Formula Allows Entrepreneurs To Retain Much of Their Autonomy," *Wall Street Journal*, 19 June 1990, B2.

28. Press release, RPM, Inc., 1 December 1986.

29. Press release, RPM, Inc., 24 October 1986.

30. www.zinsser.com.

31. "Wm. Zinsser & Co., Inc.: 150 Years of Innovation," company booklet, 1999, RPM archives.

32. "Wm. Zinsser & Co., Inc.: 150 Years of

Innovation," company booklet,1999, RPM archives.

33. "Wm. Zinsser & Co., Inc.: 150 Years of Innovation," company booklet, 1999, RPM archives.

34. "Wm. Zinsser & Co., Inc.: 150 Years of Innovation," company booklet, 1999, RPM archives.

35. "Take the Money and Stay," *FW*, 13 April 1993, 54.

36. Bob Senior, interviewed by David Patten, tape recording, 8 November 2000, Write Stuff Enterprises.

37. Bob Senior, interviewed by David Patten, tape recording, 8 November 2000, Write Stuff Enterprises.

38. Thomas Sullivan, correspondence to Jon VanZile, 8 April 2002, Write Stuff Enterprises.

39. *The Rauch Guide to the U.S. Paint Industry* (Manchester Center, Vermont: Impact Marketing Consultants, 1998), 44.

40. *The Rauch Guide to the U.S. Paint Industry* (Manchester Center, Vermont: Impact Marketing Consultants, 1998), 39–41.

41. *The Rauch Guide to the U.S. Paint Industry* (Manchester Center, Vermont: Impact Marketing Consultants, 1998).

42. "Executive's Corner," *Wall Street Transcript*, 23 June 1986, 82,298.

43. "Executive's Corner," *Wall Street Transcript*, 23 June 1986, 82,298.

44. "RPM, Inc.," *Wall Street Transcript*, 28 September 1987, 86,946.

45. Press release, RPM, Inc., 14 October 1987.

46. Joy Hakanson Colby, "By the Numbers," *Detroit News*, 10 October 2000, E1.

47. Press release, Craft House Corp., 27 August 1991.

48. "RPM buys chemical firm," *(Cleveland) Plain Dealer*, 7 September 1988, E8.

49. "CEO of the Decade," *Financial World*, 4 April 1989, 84.

50. "RPM, Inc., Acquisitions," internal document, 2 May 2000, RPM archives.

51. RPM, Inc., 1989 Annual Report.

Chapter Six:
Sidebar: Testor's

1. Bill Richards, "Secret 'Stealth' Fighter Is a Best Seller (In 12-Inch Plastic—Assembly Required)," *Wall Street Journal*, 20 August 1986, A1.

2. Roy J. Harris Jr., "But a Major Question Remains: Which Plane Is Better Designed?" *Wall Street Journal*, 17 November 1988, B1.

Chapter Seven

1. "Koppers coatings unit sold off to its managers," *Engineering News-*

Record, 13 October 1988, 22.

2. Charles Pauli, interviewed by David Patten, tape recording, 31 August 2000, Write Stuff Enterprises.

3. Charles Pauli, interviewed by David Patten, tape recording, 31 August 2000, Write Stuff Enterprises.

4. Press release, RPM, Inc., 11 September 1989.

5. Beth Belton, "'82 recession stars likely to weather '90 downturn," *USA Today*, 21 September 1990, 3B.

6. David Prizinsky, "RPM defying recession; sales may pass $500 MM," *Crain's Cleveland Business*, 4 March 1991, 6.

7. Thomas Sullivan, interviewed by David Patten, tape recording, 20 September 2000, Write Stuff Enterprises.

8. Press release, RPM, Inc., 3 December 1990.

9. Jim Karman, interviewed by David Patten, tape recording, 30 August 2000, Write Stuff Enterprises.

10. Thomas Sullivan, interviewed by David Patten, tape recording, 20 September 2000, Write Stuff Enterprises.

11. Thomas Sullivan, interviewed by David Patten, tape recording, 20 September 2000, Write Stuff Enterprises.

12. RPM, Inc., 1991 Annual Report, 12.

13. "RPM, Inc." *Value Line Investment Survey*, 3 April 1992, 525.

14. Press release, RPM, Inc., 13 December 1990.

15. RPM, Inc., 1991 Annual Report, inside cover.

16. RPM, Inc., 1992 Annual Report, 3.

17. David Prizinsky, "RPM glowing with Day-Glo purchase," *Crain's Cleveland Business*, 2 September 1991, 2.

18. "RPM, Inc.," *Value Line Investment Survey*, 3 July 1992, 525.

19. Press release, RPM, Inc., 26 March 1992.

20. Joe Ciulla, interviewed by David Patten, tape recording, 7 November 2000, Write Stuff Enterprises.

21. "RPM Carboline," memorandum from Bud Steinberg to Carboline employees, June 1992.

22. Press release, RPM, Inc., 20 July 1992.

23. Jim Karman, interviewed by David Patten, tape recording, 30 August 2000, Write Stuff Enterprises.

24. Press release, RPM, Inc., 9 October 1992.

25. Elizabeth S. Kiesche, "The secret of RPM's success: good people and good acquisitions," *Chemical Week*, 27 January 1993, 51.

26. Elizabeth S. Kiesche, "The secret of RPM's success: good people and good acquisitions," *Chemical Week*, 27 January 1993, 51.

27. Rebecca Yerak, "Those Castles Can Kill You," *(Cleveland) Plain Dealer*, 30 May 1993, 2E.

28. Press release, RPM, Inc., 8 June 1993.

29. RPM, Inc., 1994 Annual Report, 3.

30. RPM, Inc., 1995 Annual Report, 16.

31. Dave Reif, interviewed by David Patten, tape recording, 7 November 2000, Write Stuff Enterprises.

32. Press release, RPM, Inc., 26 October 1993.

33. Richard S. Teitelbaum, "Hats Off! It was a Heck of a Year," *Fortune*, 18 April 1994, 210–234.

34. Press release, RPM, Inc., 26 April 1994.

35. Hilary Durgin, "Why Rust-Oleum sale? Try theory of relativity," *Crain's Chicago Business*, 31 January 1994, 4.

36. Thomas Sullivan, interviewed by David Patten, tape recording, 31 August 2000, Write Stuff Enterprises.

37. Thomas Sullivan, interviewed by David Patten, tape recording, 20 September 2000, Write Stuff Enteprises.

38. Thomas Sullivan, interviewed by David Patten, tape recording, 31 August 2000, Write Stuff Enterprises.

39. Janet Shprintz, "Myers Hires Private Eye," *Daily Variety*, 21 January 2000.

40. Thomas Sullivan, interviewed by David Patten, tape recording, 20 September 2000, Write Stuff Enteprises.

41. Thomas Sullivan, interviewed by David Patten, tape recording, 31 August 2000, Write Stuff Enterprises.

42. Thomas Sullivan, interviewed by David Patten, tape recording, 31 August 2000, Write Stuff Enterprises.

43. Thomas Sullivan, interviewed by David Patten, tape recording, 31 August 2000, Write Stuff Enterprises.

44. Thomas Sullivan, interviewed by David S. Patten, tape recording, 31 August 2000, Write Stuff Enterprises.

45. Thomas Sullivan, interviewed by David Patten, tape recording, 20 September 2000, Write Stuff Enteprises.

46. Thomas Sullivan, interviewed by David Patten, tape recording, 31 August 2000, Write Stuff Enterprises.

47. Mike Tellor, interviewed by David Patten, tape recording, 7 November 2000, Write Stuff Enterprises.

Chapter Eight

1. "Business Briefs," *(Cleveland) Plain Dealer*, 28 January 1995, 2C.

2. "Business Briefs," *(Cleveland) Plain Dealer*, 22 March 1995, 4C.

3. "Business Briefs," *(Cleveland) Plain Dealer*, 8 July 1995, 2C.

4. "U.S. Paint Industry to Grow to $17.7 Billion by 2000," *Modern Paint &*

Coatings, February 1998, 50.

5. Press release, RPM, Inc., 24 July 1995.

6. Thomas Sullivan, interviewed by David Patten, tape recording, 20 September 2000, Write Stuff Enteprises.

7. Thomas Sullivan, interviewed by David Patten, tape recording, 20 September 2000, Write Stuff Enteprises.

8. RPM, Inc., 1995 Annual Report, 18.

9. Press release, RPM, Inc., 12 October 1995.

10. RPM, Inc., 1992 and 1997 Annual Reports.

11. RPM, Inc., 1996 Annual Report, 8.

12. RPM, Inc., 1994 Annual Report, 5.

13. Becky Yerak, "RPM, Inc., Is Looking to Expand Presence in International Markets," *(Cleveland) Plain Dealer*, 13 October 1995, 3C.

14. "RPM completes TCI Buy," *Chemical Market Reporter*, 22 January 1996, 7.

15. RPM, Inc., 1997 Annual Report, 30.

16. Press release, RPM, Inc., 22 May 1996.

17. Press release, RPM, Inc., 13 June 1996.

18. Sana Siwolop, "Taking a Shine to Rust-Oleum," *New York Times*, 13 October 1996, sec. 3, 4.

19. Karen Lane Gilsenan, "Comment—RPM, Inc.," Merrill Lynch & Co. Global Fundamental Equity Research Department, 12 March 1997,13–14.

20. Maura McEnaney, "RPM, Inc. of Medina Acquires B.F. Goodrich Unit," *Akron Beacon Journal*, 23 October 1996.

21. Joe Ciulla, interviewed by David Patten, tape recording, 7 November 2000, Write Stuff Enterprises.

22. David D. Van Tassel and John J. Grabowski, eds., *The Encyclopedia of Cleveland History*, 2nd. ed. (Bloomington, Indiana: Indiana

University Press, 1996), 1015.

23. Thomas Sullivan, interviewed by David Patten, tape recording, 20 September 2000, Write Stuff Enteprises.

24. Thomas Sullivan, interviewed by David Patten, tape recording, 20 September 2000, Write Stuff Enteprises.

25. Thomas Sullivan, interviewed by David Patten, tape recording, 20 September 2000, Write Stuff Enteprises.

26. Maura McEnaney, "RPM, Inc. of Medina Acquires B.F. Goodrich Unit," *Akron Beacon Journal*, 23 October 1996.

27. "BF Goodrich Sells Rest of Tremco to RPM," *Chemical Week*, 30 October 1996, 17.

28. "Financial Briefs," *Chemical Market Reporter*, 11 November 1996, 22.

29. "KCP acquires Tremco Window Markets Division," *Adhesives Age*, August 1997, 62.

30. "Astor Acquires Tremco's Autoglass Business," *Adhesives Age*, September 1997, 44.

31. Mary Vanac, "Ohio-based RPM Closes Deal to Buy Sealants and Coatings Maker," *Akron Beacon Journal*, 4 February 1997.

32. Jim Johnson, "RPM Seals Deal to Acquire Tremco," *(Willoughby) News-Herald*, 4 February 1997.

33. RPM, Inc., 1997 Annual Report, 5.

34. Michael Russo, "RPM & Tremco Poised for Growth," *RSI: Roofing, Siding, Insulation*, July 1997, 48.

35. Frank Sullivan II, correspondence to Jon VanZile, 8 April 2002, Write Stuff Enterprises.

36. "RPM Sells Facility to Focus on Core," *Chemical Marketing Reporter*, 2 June 1997, 22.

37. "RPM Sells Facility to Focus on Core," *Chemical Marketing Reporter*, 2 June 1997, 22.

38. Esther D'Amico, "The Entrepreneurial Finish," *Paint & Coatings Industry*, April, 1999.

39. RPM, Inc., 1997 Annual Report, 3.

40. RPM, Inc., 1997 Annual Report, 9.

41. Becky Yerak, "Doing It Up in Style," *(Cleveland) Plain Dealer*, 16 October 1997, 1C.

42. Kathie Rogers, interviewed by David Patten, tape recording, 31 August 2000, Write Stuff Enterprises.

Chapter Nine

1. Jim Karman, interviewed by David Patten, tape recording, 20 February 2001, Write Stuff Enterprises.

2. Bob Senior, interviewed by David Patten, tape recording, 11 November 2000, Write Stuff Enterprises.

3. "Rust Busting, One Gallon of Paint at a Time—Initiating Coverage," Salomon Smith Barney Holdings, Inc., 11 June 1998, 4–10.

4. RPM, Inc., 1998 Annual Report, 6.

5. Ken Evans, interviewed by David Patten, tape recording, 8 November 2000, Write Stuff Enterprises.

6. RPM, Inc., 1998 Annual Report, 6–7.

7. Sheryl Redick, interviewed by David Patten, tape recording, 20 February 2001, Write Stuff Enterprises.

8. RPM, Inc., 1998 Annual Report, 6.

9. RPM, Inc., 1998 Annual Report, 1.

10. Kathie Rogers, interviewed by David Patten, tape recording, 31 August 2000, Write Stuff Enterprises.

11. Press release, RPM, Inc., 1 July 1999.

12. Kathleen Madigan, "This Economy Has Fuel Injection," *Business Week*, 2 August 1999, 28.

13. Thomas Sullivan, interviewed by David

Patten, tape recording, 7 November 2000, Write Stuff Enterprises.

14. Ken Evans, interviewed by David Patten, tape recording, 8 November 2000, Write Stuff Enterprises.

15. Esther D'Amico, "The Entrepreneurial Finish," *Paint & Coatings Industry*, April 1999.

16. Esther D'Amico, "The Entrepreneurial Finish," *Paint & Coatings Industry*, April 1999.

17. Press release, RPM, Inc., 31 March 1998.

18. "RPM Buys Out Euclid," *Chemical Week*, 24 February 1999, 5.

19. "Medina County Protective Coatings Maker Buys English Company," *Akron Beacon Journal*, 9 July 1998.

20. Kristine Henry, "Ohio's RPM buying DAP for cash," *Baltimore Sun*, 13 July 1999, 1D.

21. Kristine Henry, "Ohio's RPM buying DAP for cash," *Baltimore Sun*, 13 July 1999, 1D.

22. RPM, Inc., 1999 Annual Report, 3.

23. RPM, Inc., 1999 Annual Report, 4.

24. RPM, Inc., 1999 Annual Report.

25. Jennifer Scott Cimperman, "Chemical Squeeze," *(Cleveland) Plain Dealer*, 12 April 2000.

26. Jennifer Scott Cimperman, "RPM Warns Profits Expected to Dip for 2000," *(Cleveland) Plain Dealer*, 12 July 2000.

27. Jennifer Scott Cimperman, "RPM Warns Profits Expected to Dip for 2000," *(Cleveland) Plain Dealer*, 12 July 2000.

28. "RPM, Inc., Reports Fiscal 2000 Results," PR Newswire, 24 July 2000.

29. Jim Karman, interviewed by David Patten, tape recording, 30 August 2000, Write Stuff Enterprises.

30. Jennifer Scott Cimperman, "No one has a crystal ball," *Houston Chronicle*, 21 August 2000.

31. Thomas Sullivan, interviewed by David Patten, tape recording, 20 February 2001, Write Stuff Enterprises.

32. Thomas Sullivan, interviewed by David Patten, tape recording, 20 February 2001, Write Stuff Enterprises.

33. Thomas Sullivan, interviewed by David Patten, tape recording, 20 February 2001, Write Stuff Enterprises.

34. Thomas Sullivan, interviewed by David Patten, tape recording, 20 February 2001, Write Stuff Enterprises.

35. Dave Reif, interviewed by David Patten, tape recording, 7 November 2000, Write Stuff Enterprises.

36. Frank Sullivan II, interviewed by David Patten, tape recording, 2 February 2001, Write Stuff Enterprises.

37. Tom Sullivan, remarks to shareholders, 12 October 2001, RPM archives.

38. Tom Sullivan, remarks to shareholders, 12 October 2001, RPM archives.

39. Ken Evans, interviewed by David Patten, tape recording, 8 November 2000, Write Stuff Enterprises.

40. Michael Zawacki, "Frank Talk," *InsideBusiness*, April 2002.

41. Michael Zawacki, "Frank Talk," *InsideBusiness*, April 2002.

42. Michael Zawacki, "Frank Talk," *InsideBusiness*, April 2002.

INDEX

Page numbers for photographs are in italics

A

Acorn Chemical Company, 57, 59, 75, 76
 decline and sale, 21–22
 founding, 12
 Frank C. Sullivan career, 12, 13–18, 20, 23
Acorn Refining. *See* Acorn Chemical Company
acquisitions. *See also* acquisition strategy; individual company names
 Agpro Limited, 107
 Alox Corporation, 58
 American Emulsions, 72
 Arr-Maz Products, 107
 Aztek Airbrush, 79
 Briggs Bros. Paint Company, 35
 Briner Paint Manufacturing Company, 79
 Carboline Argentina/Tintas Letta, 107
 Carboline Company, 68–72

Carboline Europe/Corroline, 107
Century Polymers, 83
Chemical Coatings, 81
Chemical Specialties, 75
Chemrite Coatings, 92
Compositite, 107
Conica Technik, 107
Consolidated Coatings, 76–77
Corrosion Services, 107
Craft House Corporation, 75
DAP Products, 107
Day-Glo Color Corporation, 83
Dean & Barry Company, 45, 58
Design/Craft Fabric Corporation, 58
Dryvit Poland, 92
Dryvit Systems, 89–90
Dutch Masters Paint Company, 58
Dynatron/Bondo Corporation, 84
Epoxi-Tech, 107
Espan, PTE Ltd., 90

Euclid Chemical Company, 64, 107
Eucomex, 107
Flecto Company, 107
Floquil-Polly S Color Corporation, 45
F.O. Pierce, 35–36
Gates Engineering Company, 45
Grow Chemical Corporation, 57
Guardian Products, 107
Haartz-Mason, 62
H. Behlen & Brothers, 43
Kop-Coat, 79–80
Label Systems, 76
Lindbergh Hobbies, 76
Mac-O-Lac Paints, 35
Mameco International, 59
Mantrose-Haeuser, 83
Martin Mathys N.V., 83
Mohawk Finishing Products, 42
Okura Holdings, 92
Pactra, 79
Paramount Technical Products, 79, 81

PCI Industries, 72
PLASTIC WOOD, 91
Prostruct, 107
Reardon Company, 32–34
Richard E. Thibaut, Inc., 45
Rust-Oleum, 85–87
Rust-Oleum Europe, 81–82
Simian Company, 90
Star Finishing Products, 91
Stonhard, 84
Talsol Corporation, 63
TCI, 92
Testors Corporation, 64
Toxement Holderchem, 107
Tremco, 93
Tropical Industrial
    Coatings, 57
Ultra-Tex Surfaces, 107
Westfield Coatings, 67
WOODLIFE, 90
Zehrung Corporation, 81
Zinsser, 72–74
acquisition strategy, 29,
        31–32, 36, 73–74, 84,
        91, 107. *See also*
        business strategy
Agpro Limited, 107
AGR, 62
Al Hana Mosque, 97
Alox Corporation, 58, 108
Alumanation, 10, 18, 28, 36
    expansion of sales, 22–23
    introduced by Republic
        Powdered Metals, 18
    sales leader, RPM Inc., 42,
        45, 58
    testimonial, 21
Alumanation Farms. *See*
    Brunswick Farms
American Emulsions, 72, 108
Amstutz, Dr. Max D., 83, *114*
Andrews, John, 68

annual meetings
    1979, 49, 52, 54, 56, 57
    1987, 70
    1997, 98–99
    2001, 110
Annual Report, 1996, *89*
Arco, 11–12
Armor All Products
        Corporation, 103
Armstrong, 51
Arr-Maz Products, 107
Atlantic Refining Company,
        93. *See also* Arco
automotive products, 84, 92
awards
    Business Statesman
        Award, 89
    CEO of the Decade, 75
    CEO of the Year, 79
    "E" Awards, 23, *23*, *41*, 42
    Excellence in Education
        Award, 105
Aztek airbrush, 79, 103

B

Bardamp, 15
Barron's, 47
Basic Metals, 17
Beardstown Ladies
        Investment Club, 61,
        61, 63–64
Beaver Lodge, 30, *31*
Beazer Corporation, 79
Better Investing, 49
BFGoodrich, 93
Big Orange, 42
Biltmore Hotel (Dayton, Ohio),
        17
B-I-N, 72
board of directors, 44, *52–53*,
        55–57, 61, 75, 83, *114*

Bollinger, Clayton, 55
Bondex, 32, 50, 52, 58
Bondo, 84, 109, *109*
Bondo/Mar-Hyde, 102
Bonk, Jeri, *41*
Braas GmbH, 62
Brace, Marilyn, 18, 31
Brandon, Edward, *114*
brands. *See* products and
        brands
Briggs Bros. Paint Company,
        35, 42, 50, 62
Briner Paint Manufacturing
        Company, 79
Brocksmith, Herman L., 33
Brunswick Farms, 24–25,
        24–25, 30, *31*, 37
Brush, Charles P., 84
Bulls Eye 1-2-3, *66*, 72, *73*
Bulls-I-Namel, 72
Burner, David L., 93
Business Statesman Award,
        1995, 89
business strategy, 19–21, 45,
        75, 81, 91–92. *See
        also* acquisition
        strategy; planning
        strategy
Business Week, 63
Buttoff, Clyde, 24

C

Calfee, Halter & Griswold, 37,
        44
Carboline Argentina/Tintas
        Letta, 107
Carboline Company, 96
    acquired by RPM, Inc.,
        68–72
    acquisitions, 83, 107
    reorganization, 92, 102, 108

Carboline Europe/Corroline, 107
Cartille, Frank, 20
Case Western Reserve University, 12, 33, 51
Cementseal, 15
Century Polymers, 83
CEO of the Decade Award, 75
CEO of the Year Award, 79
Chase Manhattan Bank, 45, 90
Chemgrate grating, 92
Chemical Coatings, 55, 81
Chemical Specialties, 75
Chemical Week, 79, 84, 93
Chemrite Coatings, 92
CHEMSPEC coatings, 75, 108
Chessin, James L., *78*, 96
Christmas party, 1974, *46*
Ciulla, Joe, 23, 35, 37, 83, 93
Clean Air Acts, 74
Cleary, Jack, 21
Cleveland, Ohio, 12, 104, *106*
Cleveland Athletic Club, 30
Cleveland News, 21
Cleveland Orchestra, *98*, 99
Cleveland Plain Dealer, 109
Cleveland Trust Corporation, 12, 55
Clevo Metallic Coating, 13
Coca-Cola, 75
Cofield, Charles, 72
Collins, Judy, *105*
competition, 45, 67–68
Compositite, 107
concrete additives, 64
Conica Technik, 107
Consolidated Coatings, 55, 76–77
consolidation. *See* reorganization
Consumer Division, 102–103, 108

Cook, Craig, *98*
Cook, Jan Karman, *98*
corporate officers and staff, *52–53*, 84, 96, 103, 106, *113*
Corrosion Services, 107
Cortec Group Fund, 92
Cover-Stain, 72
Covington, M.R., 49
Craft House Corporation, 75, 97
Crawford, Mary Hall, *30*, 49, 50
Culver Military Academy, 12, *14*, 27, 65
Culver Summer Naval School basketball team, *13*
Cunningham, Gardner R., 72

D

DAP Group, 108
DAP Products, *101*, *107*, 107–109
Davis, Felix, 43
Day-Glo Color Corp., 83, 102, *103*, 108
Dean & Barry Company, *39*, *43*, 45, 58, 62, 72
Deitz, Robert, 13, 55, 76–77
Design/Craft Fabric Corporation, 58
Dewey, John, 68
Dif wallpaper stripper, *67*, 76
Dillon, Read & Company, 73
divestitures, 61–62
    Auto Replacement Glass, 96
    Briggs Bros. Paint Company, 62
    Craft House Corporation, 97

Dean & Barry Company, 62, 72
Euclid Chemical Company, 82–83
F. O. Pierce, 62
Gates Engineering roof-sheeting line, 67–68
Mac-O-Lac Paints, 62
Rust-Oleum resin plants, 97
Swiggle Insulating Glass, 96
Zinsser resin plants, 97
Dividend Achiever Award, 89
Do-It-Yourself Council, 91
Dombcik, Jerry H., 84
downsizing. see reorganization
Doyle, Sr. Maureen, 104
Dryvit Poland, 92
Dryvit Systems, 89–90, 96, 102, 108
Dunn, Elmer, 34
Dun's Business Month, 63
Durabond, 107
Dutch Masters Paint Company, 58, 62
Dynatron/Bondo Corporation, 84
Dynatron brand, 84

E

"E" Award, 23, *23*, *41*, 42
earnings. *See* financial data
E-commerce Division, 106
Eiffel Tower restoration, *32*
Eisner, Michael, 75
employee benefits, 20
employee recruitment, 23
environmental issues, 74
Epoxi-Tech, 107

epoxy terrazzo floor, 92
Eriksson, Ulf, 37, *37*
Espan, PTE Ltd., 90–91
Euclid Chemical Company,
    64, 67–68, 82–83, *97*,
    107–108
Eucomex, 107
Evans, Charles M., 59
Evans, Issac, 12, 59
Evans, Kenneth M., 102–103,
    112–114
Excellence in Education
    Award, 105
expansion, 20. *See also*
    acquisitions
    Alumanation Farms,
        24–25, *24–25*, 30
    Brussels, Belgium, 20
    Cuba, 23
    Europe, 37
    Gilroy, California, 22, 24,
        37
    Hawaii, 22
    Inland Aluminum, 25
    international distribu-
        torships, 23
    Japan, 37
    Mameco, 62
    Medina, 37
    Montreal, 37
    New Jersey, 37
    St. Louis, Missouri, 37
    Toronto, 37
    West 150th Street, 19
exterior insulation and
    finishing systems, 89

F

Fergusson, Donald, 82, 86
Fibergrate Composite
    Structures, 108

Fibergrate grating, 92
Field, Walter L., 35
50th anniversary, *88*, *98*, 98–99
financial data (Republic
    Powdered Metals)
    1947, 18
    1955, 20
    1959, 24
    1963, 31
    1971, 37
financial data (RPM, Inc.)
    1971–1976, 45, 46–47
    1977–1979, 49, 58
    1980–1984, 62, 64
    1985–1989, 70, 72, 77
    1990–1994, 83, 84–85, 87
    1995–1997, 90, 99
    1998–2002, 106,
        108–109, 115
    $1 billion sales milestone,
        89, 90–91
    $100 million in sales, 59,
        61
    financial goals, 41, 83,
        113–114
Financial World, 79
Finn, Dennis, 113
Firestone Tire & Rubber, 67
Flecto Company, 107
Fleming, Bob, 15, 19–20, 25,
    27, 29, 75
Flood Company, 12
Floquil-Polly S Color
    Corporation, 45, 58
flow-control diaphragms, 62
F-19 Stealth model airplane,
    68
F. O. Pierce, 35–36, 42, 50,
    62
Forbes Varnish, 12
Ford, Gerald, 46
Fortune 500, 84

G

GACO brand, 45
Gates, Bill, 75
Gates Engineering Company,
    45, 50, 67
General Electric, 75
General Tire & Rubber, 51
George Eustis and Company,
    30
Gerace, Sam, *36*
Gibson-Homans, 12
Gigax, Les, 57, 61
Gillich, Louis, 15, 18, 29, *41*
Gilroy, California plant, 22,
    24, 42
Gilsenan, Karen, 93
Glidden, 12, 15, 16, 31, 35,
    45
Goizueta, Roberto C., 75
Gonzalez, Jose, 104
Gordon, Al, 43
Granzier, Paul A., 106
grating products, 92
Gross, Shirley, 63
Grow Chemical Corporation,
    57
Guardian Products, 107
Gustin, Lorrie, 83, *114*

H

Haartz-Mason, 62
Hammink, Niles H., 57, 61, 75
Harvard Business Club of
    Cleveland, 89
Hasman, Glenn R., 84, *113*
Hawaii Convention Center, 97
H. Behlen & Brothers, 43
headquarters (Medina, Ohio),
    43, *46*, 49–50, *50*,
    52–53, *94–95*

headquarters (West 150th Street), *19*
Heckel, George, 12
Herrmann, John, 69, 85–87
Hill, Paul H., 89
Hillman, Herbert E., 35–36, 44
hobby and craft products, 45, *63*, 64, 68, *69*, 75
Holderbank Financiere Glaris Ltd., 82–83, 107
holding company, formation of, 41
Home Depot, 100
home improvement stores, 100, *108*
Hoogenboom, Paul, 106, *113*
horse racing and breeding, 24–25
Hughes, Robert G., 75
Huston, Ruth, 61, 64
Hypalon, 45

I

Impact Marketing Consultants, 89
Industrial Division, 102–103, 108
industrial flooring, 84
Inland Aluminum, 25
InsideBusiness, 113
International Brotherhood of Electrical Workers, 11
international business, 23, 37, 42, 59, 81–82, 83, 91
Investor's Business Daily, 67
IRS audit, 23

J

Jacobus, Jack, *98*

Jacobus, Sue Sullivan, 14, *15*, 18, *22*, 40, *54*, *98*
Jansen, Piet, *78*
Johnson, Lyndon B., *23*, 23
Jones, E. Bradley, *114*
Jones, Laury, 49
Jones, Lawrence C., 57
Jones, Paul, 24
Judy, Leonard, 82
Jupiter Industries, 64

K

Karch, George, 12, 55, 61
Karlson, Axel, 64
Karman, Carol, 27, *98*
Karman, Jim, *31*, *36*, *41*, *43*, *56*, *60*, *88*, *100*, *102*, *114*
    early acquisitions, 29, 32–37
    education, 27
    family, 98
    holding company, formation of, 41, 44
    joins Republic Powdered Metals, 27
    president of RPM, 58–59
    reorganization, 1998, 102–103, 106–111
    retirement, 106, 115
    Tremco acquisition, 93
    Zinsser acquisition, 72–74
Katz, Edward M., 12, 17, 20, 57, 59
Kem-Tone, 16
Kidder Peabody, 43
Klar, Richard E., 59, 82–83, 96
Knoop, Stephen, *113*
Kop-Coat, 55, 79–80, 83, 108
Koppers Company, 79–80
Korach, Jeffrey, 64, 82, 83, 96, 111, *112*

Korach, Ken, 64
Korach, Lawrence, 64
Kugler, Herman G., 45

L

Label Systems, 76
Lehman Brothers, 69, 85–87
Lenz, Winthrop, 43
Lewis, John L., 11
Life magazine, 23
Lindbergh Hobbies, 76
Lindsay, Bruce, 70
Livingston, Jim, 33, 59, *98*
Livingston, Joan Sullivan, 14, *15*, 22, 33, 40, *54*, *98*
Lockheed, 68
Lopata, Stanley L., 68
Lowes, 100
lunch at RPM, Inc., *43*

M

Machamer, Quin, 84
Mac-O-Lac Paints, 35, 42, 50, 62
Malachi House, *106*
Mameco, 12, *48*, *97*
    acquired by RPM, 59
    expansion, 62
    Tremco Group, part of, 96, 107–108
management meeting, 1994, *78*
Mantrose-Haeuser, 83
Mar-Hyde, 63, 84
Martin, Jim, 30
Martin Mathys N.V., 83
Mary, Sister, 104
Master Mechanics, 12
Masterson, George, *17*
Matejka, Robert, *113*

Matthews, Bill, *34*
McDonald & Company, 49, 84
McLaughlin, John, 107, *112*
Medina County Gazette, 63
Medina County Travel Agency, 59
Merrill Lynch, 30, 43, 82, 92, 93
Metals Disintegrating, 17
Miami University, 12–13, 27
Microsoft, 75
Miller, Charles G., 64
Miller, Donald K., 43, 44, 70, 73–74, 114
Ministry of Public Works (Hong Kong), 23
Modern Paint and Coatings, 16
Mohawk Finishing Products, 42–43, 45, 50–51, 58
Monile, 59
Moody's Investor Service, 89, 93
Morris, Jay, 51, 59, 82–83, 93, 102–103
Municipal Light Company, 11

N

Nalco Chemical Company, 83
NASDAQ 100 Index, 89
National Association of Investment Clubs, 49, 83
National Association of Securities Dealers, 99
National City Bank of Cleveland, 33, 71
National Paint & Coatings Association, *110*
Nemeth, Julius

at Acorn Chemical Company, 15, 17–18, 20
acquisitions, role in, 29, 34
retirement, 75
vice president of beautification products, 58
Nemeth, Julius, Sr., 17
Neoprene, 45
New York, New York hotel, 90
New York Stock Exchange, 100, *100, 102*
New York Times, 99
Newborn, Isi, 25
Nixon, Richard, 42
Nullifire, 107
Nu-Sensation, 19
Nu-Tex #555, 45

O

O'Donnell, Kevin, 57
office staff, *30, 46, 102*
Ohio Cancer Research Associates dinner, *105*
Okura Holdings, 92
Old Phoenix Bank, 24
O'Neill, Dave, *98*
O'Neill, Kaki Sullivan, 14, *15*, 39, *54, 98*, 105, *106*
O'Neill, Patty, *98*
Ong, John, 93
Onoda Construction Materials, 37
operating companies. *See* acquisitions; individual company names
operating presidents, 52–53, 111, *112. See also* individual company names

P

Pabis, Connie, 42
Pabis, Frank D., 42, 44, 51, 52
Pactra, 79
Paint-by-Number art kits, 75
paint industry, 19, 47, 89
consolidation, 31
do-it-yourself market, 16
envirnomental issues, 74
World War II, 15–16
Papenbrock, William, 37, 44, *56*, 93, *114*
PaperTiger Scoring Tool, 73
Paramount Technical Products, 79
Paraseal waterproofing, 81
Pauli, Charles G., 55, 79, 103, 111, *112*
PCI Industries, 72
Pellicano, Anthony Jr., 85–87
Permaroof, 19, 23, 58
Peterman, Mary Ann, 25
Petronas Office Towers, *93*
Pettit marine products, 80, 84
planning strategy, 51–54, 82–83
Plasite Protective Coatings, 108
PLASTIC WOOD, 91
Pliable Metals Corporation, 18
PPG Industries, 12
products and brands
Alumafoil, 21
Alumanation, *10*, 18, *18*, 21, 22–23, 58
automotive products, 84, 92
Bardamp, 15
Big Orange, 42

B-I-N, 72
Bondex, 32
Bondo, 84, 109, *109*
Bulls Eye 1-2-3, *66*, 72, *73*
Bulls Eye primer-sealer, 66
Cementseal, 15
Chemgrate grating, 92
CHEMSPEC coatings, 75
Clevo Metallic Coating, 13
coatings, 45
concrete additives, 64
Cover-Stain, 72
DAP caulking, 107
Day-Glo colorants, 83, *103*
Dif wallpaper stripper, *67*, *76*
Durabond, 107
Dynatron, 84
epoxy terrazzo floor, 92
Fibergrate grating, 92
flow-control diaphragms, 62
GACO brand, 45
hobby and craft products, 45, *63*, 64, 68, *69*, 75
Hypalon, 45
industrial flooring, 84
Mar-Hyde, 63, 84
Monile, 59
Neoprene, 45
Nu-Sensation, 19
Nu-Tex #555, 45
Paint-by-Number art kits, 75
PaperTiger Scoring Tool, 73
Paraseal waterproofing, 81
Permaplastic, 21
Permaroof, 19, 23, 58
Pettit marine products, 80, 84

Ramuc swimming pool products, 80
SHIELDZ Universal Wallcovering Primer, 72
single-ply roofing sheets, 62
Superstop waterproofing, 81
Tremco sealants and coatings, *85*
Uniflex, 15, *17*, 18
Varathane wood finish, 107
Vulkem, *48*, 59
wall coverings, 45–46
Watco wood finish, 101, 107
water-based paints, 16
Weldwood, 107
Wolman wood preservatives, 80
Woolsey marine products, 80, 84
Z-Spar marine products, 80, 84
prospectus, *28*
Prostruct, 107
Purchasing Action Council, 92, 102

R

Ramuc swimming pool products, 80
Ratner, Albert, *114*
Reagan, Ronald, *79*
Reardon Company, 32–34
recessions
  1971, 41–42, 44–45, 51
  1981, 61
  1990, 80–81

2000, 108–109, 111
Redick, Sheryl, 106
Regan, Don, 43
Reif, Dave, 84, 103, 106, 110, 111, *112*
Renault, 23
reorganization, 45, 58, 96–98, 102–103, 106–111
Republic Powdered Metals, *43*, 50, 80, 96, 107, 108. *See also* financial data (Republic Powdered Metals)
  acquisitions, 29–37
  expansion and growth, 20–27
  founding, 17–18
  holding company transition, 39–41
  products, 18–20
restructuring. *See* reorganization
retail sales, 42
Rice, Ronald, *113*
Richard E. Thibaut, Inc., 45, 50, 58
Robbins, Dan, 75
Rockefeller, David, 45
Rockefeller, John D., 12
Rogers, Kathie M., 99, 106
Roller-Coater applicator, 16
Rondou, Stephan, *78*
roof coating, 15
Rose, Anthony, 72
RPM/Belgium, 108
RPM II Group, 108
RPM World Travel Inc., 59
Rubber & Plastic News, 62
Rubbermaid, 57
Rust-Oleum, *80–81*, *82*
  acquisition, 85–87, 90, 92, 97, 108

Consumer Division, part
    of, 102
and Home Depot, 100
Rust-Oleum Europe,
    80–81, 81–82
Rust-Oleum Group, 108

S

Saint Colmans school, 12
Saint Malachi Church, 104
sales data. *See* financial data
salespeople, *21*, *31*, *34*
Sanders, Samuel S., 12, 17,
    20, 57, 59
Savanuck, Daniel F., 75
Schlang, Elliott, 80
Scott & Fetzer Company, 57
Seidler, Bob, *34*
Senior, Robert, 55, 72, 100,
    111, *112*
September 11, 2001, tragedy,
    111–112
shareholder meetings. *See*
    annual meetings
Sherwin-Williams, 12, 15, 16,
    31, 35, 45, 79
SHIELDZ Universal
    Wallcovering Primer,
    72
Siebert, Jerry, 63
Siebert Associates, 63
SIFCO Industries, 57
Simian Company, 90
single-ply roofing sheets, 62,
    67, 75
Skortz, Laureen, *41*
Slade, Thomas H., 92
Smiley, Keith R., 84, *113*
Solotar, William L., 45
Spencer, Walter, 45
Spred Satin, 16

St. Louis Post-Dispatch, 33
Star Finishing Products, 91
Stavinoha, Ray, 83
Stealth fighter model, 68, *69*
Stebbins, David T., 63
Steinberg, Bud, 71, 78, 83
stockholder meetings. *See*
    annual meetings
stock offerings, *28*, *29*, 37,
    43, 58, 71
StonCor, 109
StonCor Group, 108
Stonhard, 84, 102, 108
Stork, Jeff, *78*, 84
Stranahan, Stephen, 75
Sullivan, Barbara O'Rourke,
    65
Sullivan, Charles, 11, 39
Sullivan, Dan (dog), *38*
Sullivan, Danny, *38*
Sullivan, Delphine, 11
Sullivan, Edwin, 11
Sullivan, Frank C. (father of
    Tom), *11*, *13*, *14*, *15*,
    17, *21*, *23*, *26*, *34*, *40*
  Acorn, career at, 13–18, 20
  Arco, career at, 11, 12
  birth, 11
  business strategy, 20, 22,
    29, 32, 33, 36
  death, 39–40
  education, 12–13
  family, 14, *14*, 18
  horse racing and
    breeding, 24–25
  IRS audit, 23
  Republic Powdered
    Metals, founding of, 17
  sales and marketing
    strategy, 16–17, 19–21
Sullivan, Frank C., Jr. (Sully).
    See Sullivan, Fr. Sean

Sullivan, Frank J., 11–12
Sullivan, Frank (son of Tom),
    38, 41, *65*, *113*, *114*,
    115
  birth, 27
  chief financial officer, 84
  education, 65
  executive vice president,
    91
  joins RPM, Inc., 64–65
  leadership, 112–114
  Martin Mathys
    acquisition, 83
  Tremco acquisition, 93
Sullivan, Joan. *See*
    Livingston, Joan
    Sullivan
Sullivan, John (Jack), 11
Sullivan, Julie, *38*, *105*
Sullivan, Kaki. *See* O'Neill,
    Kaki Sullivan
Sullivan, Katherine, 11
Sullivan, Kathleen, *38*
Sullivan, Margaret Jamieson,
    11
Sullivan, Mary, 91
Sullivan, Pat, 14, *15*, *19*, *22*,
    42
Sullivan, Peg, 12, 14, *15*,
    52–53, *54*
Sullivan, Sandy, *27*, *38*, *54*,
    104, *105*
Sullivan, Fr. Sean, 14, *15*, 18,
    98
Sullivan, Sean (son of Tom),
    38
Sullivan, Sue. *See* Jacobus,
    Sue Sullivan
Sullivan, Sully. *See* Sullivan,
    Fr. Sean
Sullivan, Thomas L. (brother
    of Frank C.), 11

Sullivan, Tom, *15, 29, 31, 34, 36, 38, 41, 43, 46, 49, 54, 56, 57, 60, 71, 79, 88, 100, 102, 105, 114, 115*
  acquisition strategy, 29, 32
  Annual Meeting, 2001, 110
  awards, 75, 79, 89
  birth, 14
  Carboline acquisition, 68–72
  death of father, 39–40
  early acquisitions, 32–37
  early years as president, 39–47
  education, 27
  family, 27, *38, 54, 98*
  on Frank C. Sullivan, 20
  joins Republic Powdered Metals, 27
  reorganization, 2000, 102–103, 106–111
  retirement, 106, 115
  Rust-Oleum acquisition, 81–87
  Urban Community School, benefactor of, 104–105
Sullivan, Tom, Jr., 27, *38*, 91
Sullivan, William, 11
Sun Oil, 68–71
Superstop waterproofing, 81
Swiggle Insulating Glass, 96

T

Talsol Corporation, 63, 67–68, 84
TCI, 92, 108
Technical Council, 92
Tellor, Mike, 69–70, 87, 110, *112*
testimonials, 20–21
Testor, Nils F., 64

Testors Corporation, *63*, 79, *103*, 109
  acquired by RPM, Inc., 64, 67–68
  Consumer Division, part of, 102
  F-19 Stealth model, 68, *69*
Te Vega (horse), 25
Thibaut, 50, 58
Thornton, Jerry Sue, *114*
Tinnerman, George, 13
Tompkins, P. Kelly, 106, *113*
Tongue, Ralph, 15, *41*
Toxement Holderchem, 107
trade show, *97*
Trans-Arabian Pipe Line Company, 23
Tremco, 12, *85, 93, 96*
  acquired by RPM, 93
  reorganization, 96, 102, 107
Tremco Auto Replacement Glass, 96
Tremco Group, 91, 96, 108
Tremco sealants and coatings, *85*
Treuhaft, William, 93
Tropical Industrial Coatings, 57
Tropical Paint, 12
Truman, Harry S., *26*

U

Ultra-Tex Surfaces, 107
Uniflex, 15, *17*, 18
University of North Carolina, 65
University of Wisconsin, 27
Urban Community School, 104

Ursuline Sisters, 104
USA Today, 80

V

Van Dorn Industries, 49, 57
Varathane wood finish, 107
Vetterli, John E., 107
Vulkem, 59
Vulkem 116, *48*

W

Wahlstrom, Robert, 52
Walker, G. H., 43
wall coverings, 45–46
Wall Street Journal, 68, 69, 72
Wall Street Transcript, 74
Walt Disney Company, 75
Walworth, Edward, Jr., 72
Wassall, 107
Watco wood finish, *101*, 107
water-based paints, 16
waterproofing products, 19
Web site, 106
Welch, Jack, 75
Weldwood, *101*, 107
Weltman, Clarence A., 58
Wendt, Noreen, 39
West High School, 12
Westfield Coatings, 67
Wilhelmy, C. Robert, *34, 41*
Wilhelmy, Margaret (Peg). *See* Sullivan, Peg
William Zinsser & Company. *See* Zinsser
Wise, Samuel, 12
WOODLIFE, 90
Woolman wood preservatives, 80
Woolsey marine products, 80, 84